I Shot
an Elephant
in My Pajamas

by Morrie Ryskind
with John H. M. Roberts

HUNTINGTON HOUSE PUBLISHERS

Huntington House Publishers
P.O. Box 53788
Lafayette, Louisiana 70505

Library of Congress Card Catalog Number 93-77474
ISBN 1-56384-000-6

Cover Idea by: Karen A. Theriot

Dedication

For Mary

Top (Left to Right)
Ira and George Gershwin
Bottom (Left to Right)
George S. Kaufman and Morrie Ryskind

The Gershwins and Kaufman were Ryskind's main collaborators during his lay career.

CONTENTS

CHAPTER ONE

A playwright whose works I've always held in high regard once wrote: "all the world is a stage." That being stated, my entrance took place in Brooklyn on 20 October 1895. This a distinction (the location—let's skip over the date) that I've always cherished, as it makes me constitutionally eligible to be elected to the presidency. At this stage of my life, I'm beginning to concede, regretfully, that the possibility of that happening is looking rather doubtful. But then again, stranger things have happened. For instance, I recently received a letter from Bill Buckley, and there wasn't a single word in it that sent me to the dictionary. (Either he's slipping, or I finally have something to show for all those crossword puzzles.)

My life, should any presidential kingmakers be taking note, began in a two-room apartment on the top floor of a five-story walkup tenement in the Williamsburg section of Brooklyn. The building was bereft of gas, electricity, heat, and telephones, and had a plumbing system which consisted of a communal hand pump on the first floor and a row of rat-infested privies in the back alley. And that, by my reckoning, is the Jewish equivalent of a log cabin on the frontier.

With our neighborhood being predominantly Jewish, I learned to speak Yiddish as my first language. Both of my parents were from the Byelorussia province of Russia, and as was the case with so many immigrants in New York at that time, they had lived within a stone's throw of each other in the old country but didn't meet until they arrived in America.

It was the era when a rumor about Jews using Christian blood in the preparation of matzohs kicked off the Czarists pogroms. My parents were lucky to get out of Russia alive. Many of my relatives didn't. The population of the village that one of my cousins lived in suffered a near-total annihilation. My cousin escaped by smearing blood on his shirt and pretending to be dead. When darkness fell, he escaped into the woods, started running, and didn't stop until he hit Flatbush Avenue.

My parents, Abraham and Ida, were a colorful contrast to each other, and in remembering them, it's easy to spot the bifurcated nature of my career. The many years that I spent in show business can be attributed to my mother. She was a natural-born jokester who could amuse herself for hours by singing the nonsensical songs from the Yiddish theaters which she frequented with a regularity that bordered on a religious commitment. My enduring fascination with politics can be traced to my industrious, sober-minded father, whose passions in life were working fourteen to sixteen hours a day, thrift, and talking back to the editorials in his evening newspaper.

Aside from the love that they had for each other and their children, the strongest bond that my parents shared was their pride in being Americans. In our age of wealth and cynicism, the inherent ethos of the American dream is pretty much taken for granted, if not disregarded altogether, but to my parents, despite the harshness of their early circumstances, America offered them a new hope and a new language; both of which they eagerly embraced.

In the latter portion of my career as a columnist, one matter that I frequently felt compelled to take issue with (rail against would probably be a better choice of words), was a bill passed by the California State Legislature that required all ballots, as if they weren't long enough already, to have their instructions printed bilingually. Being that the Declaration of Independence and the Constitution were printed in the King's English, it seemed to me that which was good enough for the founding fathers should also serve us equally well.

Such a stance brought me a rash of reader responses, most of which came by mail, but one of my more determined anonymous, anathematic correspondents managed to obtain my unlisted phone number, the result being that I had to have it changed yet another time, and that I had to make several trips to the otologist's office to have the venom dug out of my ear.

For three minutes or so, he directed at me, without repeating himself, a veritable anthology of graffiti, ranging from four-letter words to hyphenated 12-letter ones, including several anatomical suggestions that defied all the laws of both biology and physics. One of his few quotable charges was that I was a "myopic, bigoted troglodyte." Considering my optomical problems, "myopic" is not far from the truth. I've come to accept that to a large portion of the liberal community, "troglodyte" is the going synonym for conservatism, but being labelled as a "bigot" bristled the follicles of my long-since departed hair. If the allegation were true, then it would also have to apply to how I felt about my parents, and the folly of that line of reasoning speaks for itself.

When my parents arrived in America, neither of them could speak a word of English, but through hard work and night school, they eventually conquered both the spoken and written language of their new home. My father was a very proud man, and it must have been hard on him to have to study from the same grammar school textbooks that I was using, but it was necessary, and when he passed his citizenship examinations, he proclaimed it to be the proudest day of his life.

My parents came to America during the age of sweatshops and immigrant exploitation. Unskilled as a laborer and unable to speak English, my father spent his first few years in America working twelve hours a day, six days a week, in a garment factory at sixty-five cents a day. In an effort to save what little there was of his pay, he slept on a cot in the boiler room of an office building where he stoked the furnaces at night in lieu of paying rent. By the time he married, he had managed to save up (don't ask me how) enough money to buy a streetcorner kiosk where he sold newspapers, cigarettes, and candy. His hours certainly weren't any better, but he was his own boss, and the little enterprise was modestly profitable, which was of no small consequence to a man whose worldly possessions just a few years earlier had consisted of the contents of one suitcase.

Our standard of living during those years when we lived in Brooklyn was marked by very few comforts and a great deal of hope. Any extra penny that wasn't needed for essential provisions was earmarked for that day when we would be able to buy our way out of poverty.

The only time that my father didn't work was Sunday afternoons. On that day, we would walk to a little park at the base of Brooklyn Bridge. It was quite a long walk for us, but the discomfort was eased by the fact that had we taken a trolley car, the round trip fare for two adults and a child would have set our liberation fund back by twenty-four cents. At the park, I would play with the other children while my mother sat on a bench and talked quietly with the women from our building. My father would join the men who stood at the railing which prevented anyone from falling down the short rocky incline into the bay. There was very little talking done between them. They would simply stand there for hours looking out across the water at the skyline (considerably lower then) of Manhattan. So acute was their desire to be a part of that new world with all of its heralded greatness, and so oppressive was their sense of captivity in Brooklyn, that in my childish fantasy, the reality of our unpleasant circumstances fused with my religious instructions until I believed that a latter-day Moses would come along some day, part the East River, and lead the Jews out of Brooklyn.

For our family, the long-awaited exodus took place in the summer of 1900. We packed our belongings into a rented wagon, on top of which I took my perch, and clip-clopped our way across the bridge into the city where it was reputed that the streets were paved with gold, and lunch was served for free.

When we came off the bridge into lower Manhattan, my heart sank with the sort of crushing alacrity of which only the truly innocent are capable. The streets of the slum we had entered were most definitely not paved with gold but were in fact every bit as crowded, dirty, and oppressive as the slum neighborhood that we had just left. Fortunately, my fears were short-lived, and when I learned that Washington Heights wasn't located on the Lower East Side, my despair lifted by degrees, corresponding to each block that we passed in our uptown progression.

When we finally reached our new home on West 145th Street, I couldn't have been more thrilled if we had somehow or another contrived to inherit all of the riches from the Arabian Nights. Our apartment had three rooms, steam heat, electricity, and hot running water, which from my perspective, put us on a socio-economic plane with Rockefeller, Harriman, Morgan, Vanderbilt, Fitch, and Frick.

Washington Heights at that time was a quiet community of small businesses where the butcher, baker, barber, cobbler, druggist, and saloonkeeper knew everyone by their first names. It was an attractive neighborhood of newly constructed brownstones and tree-lined streets, and there were still in existence then many two-storied houses, most of which were the former summer homes of the city's wealthy residents dating back to Civil War era when upper Manhattan was regarded as "out in the country." The idea of street crime seemed as far-fetched as science fiction then, which made walking about and visiting one's neighbors after dark a normal part of everyday life. All in all, it was a wonderful place in which to grow up during the early years of this century. Today it's known as the cocaine capital of the world. I love progress.

Until his family moved away, my best friend in Washington Heights was a boy named Jack Smith. We played a lot of baseball together on Riverside Drive which was still unpaved then. As it was only the beginning of the automobile age, we could play there without having to stop for a passing car more than two or three times during an entire afternoon.

The Smith family was going through a rough period then. They had moved to New York from Canada following the death of Jack's father. Mrs. Smith was working in the neighborhood at whatever jobs she could find, but it was Jack's older sister (by two years), Gladys, who was the family bread-winner. Gladys was a child actress who had started traveling around the country in touring productions when she was six-years-old. She was an exceptionally mature and self-reliant child who thought nothing of handling her own traveling and lodging arrangements and mailing home a weekly paycheck at an age when most girls were still playing with dolls.

Little Gladys became my first love, but it was a love that was to remain unrequited, as I only had occasion to see her on two of the short visits that she made with her family before they relocated. Even though our encounters were brief, the angelic aura that was projected by the sweetness of her smile and the glow of her golden curls was enough to reduce my eight-year-old heart to a mass of quivering jelly. I may have been the first boy to have had a crush on her, but I certainly wasn't the last. A few years later, little Gladys was to become "America's Sweetheart" when she changed her name to Mary Pickford.

Our move to Washington Heights was the result of my father having made a down payment on a small store that was on the first level of an office building at the end of our block. It was the sort of neighborhood mom-n-pop operation that has pretty much gone out of existence today. A person could buy just about any kind of merchandise there, but its chief attraction was the variety of newspapers that my father carried.

With the commercial debut of radio and television still several decades in the distance, most people at the time received their news and opinions from the newspaper. There were around fifteen major papers in New York then, several neighborhood publications, and at least a dozen foreign language dailies. I had started to work around my father's newsstand in Brooklyn when I was three-years-old and continued to do so when we moved to Washington Heights. Several times each day, I would pull my wagon, or sled, depending on the weather, to the various trolley car stops where the newspaper bundles were thrown off. By having to be able to recognize the correct mastheads, I began to associate the letters of the alphabet with words. This led to an association of words to sentences, and in the process, I taught myself to read. Quite well as it turned out, so much so, that when I entered the first grade, I was able to pass a reading proficiency test on the sixth-grade level.

Reading became the first true passion of my life. When the bad weather of those endless winter months curtailed outdoor activities, I was quite content to stay in my bedroom poring over every book that I could borrow from the library of P.S. 186. I was especially attracted to the verse of Homer, Kipling, and Shakespeare. By the time I was ten, I had devoured all of their collected works, and to that distinguished troika do I attribute the acquisition of eyeglasses as a permanent part of my ensemble.

I was fascinated by words and their power, be it for good or evil, and of their usage. During the Christmas break of my seventh-grade year, I read the dictionary from cover to cover. It had suddenly occurred to me one day that if a person wanted to become a writer, all the tools of his trade were contained in that one book. All one had to do was to learn how to arrange them in proper sequence, somewhat as in a game of dominoes. Subsequent experiences in my career have given me cause to smile at the basic premise of my theory. Nevertheless, the origins of my career as a writer can be traced back to that day when I read the last letter *Z* in my *Webster's* and felt as if I had unlocked one of the greatest mysteries of life.

During the warm weather months, the world of literature was easily surrendered to some memorable first-hand explorations and adventures. On my ninth birthday, the city of New York opened its first subway, the West Side IRT. Since its northern terminus happened to be at the end of our block on 145th Street, I couldn't help but feel that it was all in my honor and was deeply grateful to Mayor McClellan for the present.

After the subway was commissioned, a nickel would get me to any part of our ethnically diversified city in less than half an hour—sometimes to my regret. The Irish kids of Hell's Kitchen were an especially belligerent lot, and for an "uptown Sheenie," wandering onto their turf meant either a fight or a flight to safety. I was a pretty good runner in those days.

Under normal circumstances, I would have been happy to give the hooligans a wide berth—once beaten, twice shy—but I had no choice but to traverse through their ghetto in order to reach the adjacent Jewish ghetto where my sainted grandfather lived in such contentment near his synagogue. Grandpa was a strapping six-footer with a beard that was nearly as long as he was tall. Being that he was an old-worlder and heavily steeped in the Jewish traditions, I was put under his tutelage when it came time for my bar mitzvah. (This being, at least according to Russian beliefs, the ceremony when Jewish boys mark the sprouting of horns from our foreheads.)

Once a week, Grandpa and I would go over all of the ancient covenants and biblical teachings. This was a pretty turgid way to spend an afternoon, although the part about Solomon and his three hundred wives and eight hundred concubines could certainly set the imagination spinning into tantalizing possibilities. I mean, let's face it, getting a date on Saturday night was not one of this guy's big problems. I kept my tongue, and probably would have made it all the way through my lessons unscathed had it not been for the Tower of Babel. What I should have done when Grandpa queried me about the reason for its incompletion was give a solemn account about the confusion of tongues. What I did, was pop off about a scandal involving the Plain of Shinar's stone and mortar contractors taking kickbacks. This resulted in a whacking that made the Irish kids look like creampuffs.

Happily, New York could offer quite a few other diversions besides the Lower East Side. Teddy Roosevelt was president from 1901 to 1909, and catching a glimpse of the hero of San Juan Hill as he changed trains for Oyster Bay was always a valid reason for skipping school. The legendary Houdini was forever being straightjacketed and encased in vaults, submerged in the river or suspended upside down from tall buildings, only to escape death with a regenerative power that is seldom seen outside the parameters of TV cartoons, and he too was cause for several truancy marks on my report cards.

It was also the time when powered flight was in its infancy, and the name most closely associated with the early aviation headlines was Barney Oldfield, who was already famous for setting automobile speed records that surpassed an unbelievable 60 mph. When I was in the eighth grade, it was rumored that there was to be a flying exhibition around the New York harbor one day. A group of us who had never seen an airplane before was naturally compelled to skip school to witness the event. In hopes of getting a ringside seat, we took the ferry out to the Statue of Liberty. It was possible to walk up and out onto the observation deck of her torch then, but when we got there, the privilege had already been appropriated by a

party of political big shots. We were forced to watch from
the retaining wall at the end of the island, and when the
airplane circled low over the water, we waved to the pilot
who waved back. Exciting though the aviation novelty
was, we were greatly disappointed to learn that the pilot
wasn't the daring racecar driver Barney Oldfield, but
some unheard-of bicycle mechanic from Ohio named
Wilbur Wright.

There was a host of other heroes to turn a boy's head
then, but my greatest adulation was reserved for those
intrepid players who suited up as the New York Giants.
Before their Iscariotic move to San Francisco in the 1950s,
the Giants played at the Polo Grounds, a scant fifteen
minute walk from my home on West 145th Street, or a
four minute sprint from P.S. 186. A steep hill known as
Coogan's Bluff overlooked the Polo Grounds, and it was
there that I would run every day after school during the
season and climb up into a tree for a bird's-eye view of a
game or a practice session.

The men who filled out the Giants' roster then—Iron
Man McGinty, Red Jack Murray, Bugs Raymond, Turkey
Mike Donlin, Moose McCormick, Buck Herzog, Rube
Marquand, and Bonehead Merkle—had an enviable element of male rankness about them. They were a profane,
pugnacious, swaggering, inebriated, tobacco-spitting lot
who seemed to spend about as much time brawling on
the infield as they did in the actual playing of the game.
Many of them were pulling down annual salaries that
surpassed the astronomical sum of $5,000, and when they
went on the road, they always traveled in first-class Pull-
mans and stayed at the best hotels. They also didn't seem
to have any trouble attracting girls, a particular which was
beginning to take on more and more importance in my
life then.

Whenever I wasn't daydreaming about girls, I could
usually be found daydreaming about the day when I
would be a major league pitcher (which, in my daydreams,
always helped me get girls). For role models, I selected

two legendary Giants: Iron Man McGinty and Christy Mathewson. McGinty had a fastball that was rather slow by most standards, and he was never a strikeout king, but he had one pitch with a rising arc to it that was all but impossible to hit with anything other than the edge of the bat. That pitch, combined with his double-header stamina, resulted in more pop-ups than any other major leaguer that I've ever seen. Mathewson had two specialties: a knuckleball which he tagged a "dry spitter" that blurred through the air only to lose momentum and drop away in front of the batter's box, and a "fadeaway throw" that was actually a reverse curve. After a lot of experimentation, I came up with a pitch that combined Mathewson's fadeaway throw and the Iron Man's rising arc. It was never destined to be recorded on a bubblegum card, but it helped me win a lot of games on Riverside Drive.

It was my patrilineage which proved to be the undoing of all my dreams of an enshrinement at Cooperstown. Throughout grade school I was of normal size, but as I made the transition into adolescence, I realized, to my horror, that I had—as had my father and his antecedents— peaked at 5'5", while my classmates (which made me feel as if I were shrinking) continued to shoot up around me.

Determined to triumph over what I felt to be the cruelty of nature, I entered into a Spartan regime that would have, in an earlier time, gained me entrance into the warrior's circle of Apache Indians. For years, I indulged myself in an orgy of calisthenics, vitamin pills, early retirements, and triple helpings of every vegetable dish that I could force down my throat without gagging. Despite having eaten enough spinach to empower an entire navy of Popeyes, not to mention all of the other excesses of my delusive program, my physique retained an appearance that was not unlike that of the bony, bespectacled nebbish in the TV commercial who is ambushed by a pack of bikinied bacchanals over the sight of a manufacturer's label on his swim trunks.

In addition to the emotional discombobulation result-

ing from my truncated growth, I also encountered all of
the various obligatory traumas associated with adolescence, but for the main part, my early years were a very
enjoyable time. My sisters, Sally, Mary, and Ruth, were
born after we moved to Washington Heights, raising our
family's size to a happy half-a-dozen. All of us pitched in
around my father's store, which helped to insure the
success of its operation.

My father sought to compensate all of us for the years
of deprivation that we had endured while living in Brooklyn by providing the family with the latest in twentieth
century creature comforts. However, the traditions of his
Old World upbringing were too deeply ingrained in him
to allow him to ever purchase anything until he could pay
for it in cash. For that reason, we were the last family in
our neighborhood to own, among other things, a hand-
cranked victrola, which was the 1905 version of a home
entertainment center.

My mother's greatest enjoyment arising out of our
improved standard of living was that it allowed her to
frequent the neighborhood Yiddish theater on a regular
basis. The first show that I can remember accompanying
my mother to was a benefit performance by Will Rogers.
Normally he would headline at one of the large vaudeville
theaters downtown, but on this occasion he had volunteered his services to help raise funds for some immigrant children who had been orphaned. His one-liners
and rope tricks were greatly appreciated, but the highlight of the evening came when he delivered a long
monologue in Yiddish. It was a superb piece of showman-
ship, the effect of his "Oi Veys" delivered in that inimitable Oklahoma drawl built on top of the other until the
tiny theater was nearly laughed off its foundation. There
are few narcotics in this world that are stronger than
laughter and applause, and I'm quite sure that the seeds
of my addiction with show business were planted that
night.

As I got a bit older, and my mother's fluency in

English improved, we began making trips downtown to the professional theaters in the Longacre Square area (renamed Times Square in 1904, due to the auspices and proximity of the newly erected New York Times Building). Victorianism still maintained a stranglehold over the social order of the day, and as one of its strongest bastions was the theater, we wound up more often than not sitting through a melodrama. The plays, which were illuminated by gas lamps and performed before painted one-dimensional backdrops, were archly written morality tales replete with feigning ingenues whose virtue was constantly being threatened by the nefarious schemes of black-mustachioed bounders. Virtue inevitably won out in the end, aided along by a considerable amount of hissing at the lecherous Lothario from those of us in the audience.

The classics, especially Shakespeare, were enjoying an especially strong vogue then, and they too were performed in a laughably archaic manner characterized by a grand assault of sweeping gestures, posturing and bellowing. One of the greatest practitioners of that silver exclamatory school of classical emoting was Richard Mansfield, whose legendary talent was matched, if not surpassed, only by his legendary ego. Self-absorbed to the point of self caricature, he was shamelessly supercilious in his regard for the opinions of the general public, and even more so in his treatment of his fellow actors, most of whom he would not lower himself to speak to off the stage.

I only had the opportunity to see two of Mr. Mansfield's on-stage performances, but off stage he performed his favorite role for a group of us from Washington Heights nearly every afternoon during the summer. He lived in an elegant townhouse in the West 70s, from which he could venture forth in the afternoons for an automobile outing on Riverside Drive. Being a great believer in the prerogatives of aristocracy, he was contemptuous of anything that might impede his way, such as speed limits, traffic signals, and pedestrians. Rounding the curve where our baseball game was in progress, he would bear down on us with a wide-open accelerator while thundering out, "Filthy urchins! Avant and quit my sight!" We would scatter for our lives, swearing revenge each time, but before a plan could ever be conceived and executed, the "sweet prince" made his final exit from the world's stage—sung to his rest, no doubt, by flights of angels.

Still and all, for all of its absurdities and pretensions, I became entranced with the energy and magic that pulsated from those few square blocks of the theater district, and by the time I entered into high school I knew with complete certainty that I wanted to be a playwright.

Having maintained a high scholastic average during grammar school, I sought after and obtained a scholarship to Townshend Harris Hall, which seemed the logical first step toward the attainment of my newly discovered career goals. This was a private school, long since defunct, that prepared students for admittance to City College.

Participating in the advanced academic curriculum at "THH" meant that we were allowed to study Greek, which I loved, and compelled to take philosophy, which I loathed. My natural dislike of the subject was compounded by the droning lectures of a monotoned misanthrope of such dour extremes that compared to him, Hamlet seemed like Scaramouche. Saturated to the point of rebellion, I once defied completing his homework assignment and substituted a composition titled "What Is It We're Making When We're Not Making Love?", for which I spent four consecutive Saturdays sitting in the detention hall.

Draconian measures aside, I will be forever grateful to Townshend Harris Hall, as it was there that I had my first exposure to Gilbert & Sullivan, who were to have an enormous impact on my professional life. I was amazed at how savagely they could satirize the mores and manners of the British government and society, and yet do it in a style of such obvious love and respect. So great was my regard for their works that whenever my allowance

wouldn't stretch far enough to allow me to purchase a
new phonograph of their operettas, I would forego all of
my trips to the Polo Grounds until I had accumulated the
necessary funds.

To the great agony of my family, who were constantly
inventing new excuses to leave the apartment, and our
neighbors who were forever pounding on our walls, stomp-
ing on our ceiling, or thumping against our floor with
broom handles, I replayed my G & S record collection
until I knew each of those librettos by heart. With William and Arthur looking over my shoulder, I began turning out light verses of my own. These early efforts were
submitted to and accepted by such magazines as *Puck and
Pictorial Review*, whose royalty checks of twenty-five cents
a poem gave me the dizzying distinction of being a professional writer. My sense of chutzpah, quite healthy in its
natural state, expanded even further with each new acceptance. When I had sold about fifty poems to the small
magazines, I summoned up all the courage in my fifteen-
year-old body and mailed off my first contribution to
F.P.A.

From the early teens until the early forties, Franklin
P. Adams' "The Conning Tower" was a hugely popular
literary column. "The Conning Tower," which ran for
nearly a decade in the *Herald Tribune*, a decade in the
New York World, and thereafter in the *Herald*, was a general interest column noted for the merit of its literary
style. Adams did most of the writing himself, but a small
cadre of humorists including George S. Kaufman, Marc
Connelly, Alexander Woollcott, James Thurber, Newman
Levy, Dorothy Parker, Robert Benchley, and myself became frequent contributors. There was never any pay
involved, but our regard for Adams and the prestigious
standards that he established was such that all of us continued to make contributions to "The Conning Tower"
long after we were established in our own careers.

For the most part, I contributed light verse, which
Adams, an accomplished poet himself, was very fond of.

During the summer between my junior and senior years at Townshend Harris Hall, cheeky lad that I was, I wrote an entire column, which Adams, who was very athletically oriented (it was he who had immortalized the Chicago Cubs' double play artists with his ballad "Tinkers to Evers to Chance"), printed in its entirety so as to relieve himself of that day's duties and gained himself an extra session on the tennis courts.

The notoriety that was accorded to me, a mere high-school student who had substituted for the famous F.P.A., brought me some very welcome recognition in the Washington Heights area—especially from the neighborhood girls, who previously tended to look at any boy who didn't have a varsity letter sewn to the front of his jacket as if he were invisible. In addition to making further contributions to "The Conning Tower" during my senior year, I made a concentrated effort at studying, which resulted in my becoming the class valedictorian. For the commencement address, I delivered the declaration from Xenophon in Greek, and that achievement plus my association with "The Conning Tower" brought me congratulatory telegrams from several celebrities, including the mayor, and a slew of flattering notices in the newspapers.

In retrospect, it would seem that I had chalked up some pretty impressive credits for a seventeen-year-old, but the faded entries from my daily journal of that year now read like the lamentations of Job. I felt ready to conquer the world. "Why," I kept asking myself, "was the world so slow in acquiescing? Let us all sigh for the impatience of youth."

CHAPTER TWO

As the publisher of the *New York World*, Joseph Pulitzer's refinement of yellow journalism made him a fantastically wealthy man. Along with a number of other notable robber barons of that era, Pulitzer's conscience compelled him to spend his final years atoning for a lifetime of avarice with staggering acts of philanthropy. Carnegie, Ford, and Rockefeller all had their foundations; Pulitzer had his school of journalism. Largely through Pulitzer's reputation, the state of journalism was such at that time that old Joe had quite a time trying to buy his way into respectability. Starting with Harvard, school after school in the Ivy League refused to accept his 2 million dollar endowment. Columbia finally took him in, but only after further distancing itself from Pulitzer by insisting that the school wouldn't open until the great muckraker had died. This took place in 1911, and when the Columbia University School of Journalism opened two years later, I took a pleasant twenty minute stroll down Broadway and enrolled in its first class.

There were seventy-seven of us in the class of 1917, or 17J as we took to calling ourselves, and among our distinguished group could be found: George Sokolsky, who was to become one of the most widely-read political columnists in the country; Max Schuster, who was to co-found the Simon and Schuster publishing firm; and

Merryle Rukeyser, long regarded as the dean of America's financial writers.

The most colorful member of our class was the legendary Herman Mankiewicz, with whom I maintained an on-again/off-again friendship. I take some pride in that fact, as Mank was not the easiest of fellows to get along with, and more than a few of his friendships ended up in the off column. Why he felt that his mission in life was to be the irritant in the oyster I can't say, but I do remember that whatever the topic of the discussion—academic, political, or religious—Mank would hurl his formidable intelligence against the conventional line for the pure hell of it. And the more passionately that a person clung to a cherished belief, the harder Mank would hound him until tempers flared.

The method of Mank's needling could also come in other forms, but the results were the same. A good deal of it seemed to be directed at me, and one day my temper flared up while we were sitting in anthropology class. Mank, who was sitting in the seat behind me that term, took to relieving his boredom (he once interrupted a lecture to interject: "This is all very interesting, but wouldn't it be more useful if someone figured out how all those Jews got into New York?") by placing his left foot on top of his desk and tapping my shoulder with the toe of his shoe. I'd tell him to stop, and he would for awhile, before starting up again. Then I'd turn around and knock his foot to the floor and again, there would be a cessation before the tapping resumed.

Toward the end of the term, the time came when I had had enough. When the tapping started one morning, I stood up, wheeled around, and popped Mank a good one on his rather prominent snout. My punch was no threat to the Dempsey legacy, but it was sufficient enough to send Mank from the room dripping blood. Needless to say, that action brought the class to a stunned halt and I fully expected to be sent packing to the dean's office. The classroom is no place for fisticuffs, and on that part of the issue I was truly ashamed of myself. But when I turned around to face Dr. Compton, he merely said, "Thank you," and I sat down, and the lecture continued.

It was quite a while before Mank would speak to me after that incident, and then just as we became friends again, the friendship was off again. This was due to Mank's Falstaffian (even in school) nature. Always strapped for money, he got his pocket change by turning his dormitory room into an erotic reading library where, for a dollar an hour, one could palpitate over banned copies of *Fanny Hill* and *The Memories of Josephine Mutzenbacher*. This money, and there was a steady supply of it, would promptly be lost on long-odds wagers. Because of this I wrote of him in the *Jester*:

> I'll say this much for H. J. Mank,
>
> When anybody blew, he drank.

Time has a way of smoothing ruffled feathers and I'm happy to say that there were to be very few off periods during the rest of our long friendship.

The classmate with whom I was the closest was Howard Dietz.

Howard was the product of Russian immigrants who had settled in Washington Heights. As classmates at Townshend Harris Hall, we co-edited the school paper and played a lot of baseball. While at Columbia, Howard began making contributions to F.P.A.'s column, signing himself "Freckles," which he had in abundance then. After graduation, Howard had a long and bountiful career as a stage and screen writer with hits such as *The Bandwagon* and *Three's a Crowd*.

In his memoir, *Dancing in the Dark*, Howard was to write of me,

> He was an opponent of the fraternity system and hated the reactionaries who were particularly prevalent in the Ivy League. Even though his politics were left of center, he kept the campus amused. He was active in all election debates and made rude speeches

in front of Hamilton Hall. Released from the confines of the University, he started leaning to the right,
and later became a champion of Joe McCarthy.

To those of you to whom I am known primarily
through my political writings of recent years, Howard's
remembrance—"his politics were left of center . . ."—may
come as a surprise. It's been said of me that my life
validates the ancient theory about youthful radicals evolv-
ing into late-in-life conservatives. It's a theory which I am
happy to embrace, as it means that all of those baby
boomers who protested their way through the sixties (the
crowd from Columbia especially comes to mind) will be
carrying the banner of conservatism into the new millen-
nium.

In regard to the radical (in retrospect it does seem the
correct word) behavior of my student days, I can attribute
part of it to adolescent idealism, but the majority of the
credit (or blame) is due to the fact that the city of New
York at that time was a place where promulgating opinions was a natural extension of daily life.

Tammany Hall was running the city then and had a
"captain" living on each block who knew the affairs of
each household as well as any family member. Turkeys
would be distributed to the poor on holidays, jobs would
be found for the unemployed, and company would be
provided for the shut-ins, and on election day, debts
would be repaid accordingly. It was an all enveloping
process, and few were exempt from its reach. In later
years when I was in Philadelphia with the out of town
tryouts for *Animal Crackers*, Sam Harris (the show's producer) and I returned to New York to vote on election
day. Sam accompanied me to my precinct and then I
accompanied him to his en route to catching the train
back to Philadelphia. Everyone seemed generally surprised
when Sam entered the precinct. When Sam explained
that he had come to cast his vote, a ward boss pulled him
aside and said apologetically, "Sam, you didn't have to go
to all this trouble. We knew that you were out of town,
so we went ahead and voted for you."

Although the Tammany gang maintained a stranglehold on the city, there would always be reform candidates and fusion tickets coming forth to challenge its power. Candidates would simply appear in the neighborhood, usually after suppertime, and although I never actually saw anyone stand on a soapbox, I can vividly recall dozens of impromptu debates conducted from the stoops of various brownstones on our street.

As most of my Columbia classmates were from New York and had likewise been exposed to street politics all of their lives, it tended to make 17J a very argumentative class. Columbia sought to foster an image of itself as an enlightened academic setting, which greatly facilitated our transition from an interest in local to world politics. The issue of capital and labor was continuously debated, fueled by the theories advanced by guest speakers ranging from Samuel Gompers to Eugene Debs, when the latter wasn't running for president.

Although we patterned our lives after the student radicals of France and Germany of the 1840s, it was not done to the exclusion of the normal interests and pursuits of a young man in the green-gold springtime of his years. Columbia sought to improve my brain, but nearby Barnard College nurtured my heart.

That was the time when girls wore long skirts with high-buttoned shoes, lace blouses with leg-of-mutton sleeves, wide-brimmed hats resting on Gibson Girl hairstyles, and chokers, usually black velvet with an embossed cameo, which, to this day, I regard as the most sensuous item that a girl can wear. It was an ensemble which provided an effect of grace and refinement that inspired me to spend countless hours searching for faces in clouds and churn out hundreds of heartfelt verses, from which (love has its practical side, too) I was able to derive my spending money by selling an occasional one to a magazine.

When money ran right, New York could still be an enchanting place for young love. There were long walks and picnics in the park, but my fondest memories are of those warm evenings spent riding the open-air, double-deckered buses, which sadly have gone the way of the Polo Grounds and Ezmerelda's Lemon Lime Soda Fizz. For a dime, two people could board in Washington Heights and spend a thoroughly enjoyable hour majestically enthroned on the upper level, marveling at the city's unparalleled skyline and streetlife, as the bus made its way down Broadway to the Village. For a nickel, an ice cream soda could be shared, and another dime would purchase the return-home fare. Such was the life with us, the two-bit lovers.

An evening out with my classmates proved to be a bit more expensive, and a great deal more arduous. Unlike Shakespeare's Old Adam, I can't say that "In my youth I never applied hot and rebellious liquors to my blood." Along with what I would guess to be a great proportion of college men from all eras, we foolishly used drinking as a competitive measure of our manhood. Our excessive bouts with "the evil of drink"—as it was referred to by the prohibitionists who frequently picketed the front entrance—were conducted at the Lion Saloon which was located at Broadway and 110th Street.

Alcoholic overindulgences can exact a terrible revenge, but we circumvented nature by sleeping on our right sides, a trick whose discovery probably had its origins with prehistoric man, but, when it was in vogue with our crowd at the Lion, was being attributed to the hard-drinking Cossacks of Ivan the Terrible. If one sleeps on one's back, stomach or left side, the alcohol trapped in the stomach will continue to be reabsorbed into the bloodstream, resulting in the subsequent nausea and hangover. If, however, one sleeps on the right side where the entrance to the large intestine is located, the alcohol drains from the stomach, allowing one to rise the following morning with a relative amount of impunity. I'm somewhat reluctant to go on record espousing that sort of information, but had we not known of it, a goodly portion of 17J would have fallen by the wayside.

One of my classmates' favorite escapades was to meet somewhere in the Village and drink their way back to Columbia, by taking one belt in each saloon along Broadway, which was no small trick, as there was a bar on nearly every corner. My one and only involvement with this madness happened on a night when a group of us had gone down to a small theatre on MacDougal Street to see an evening of one-act plays by an up-and-coming playwright named Eugene O'Neill. After the performance, we walked to Broadway and ordered our first drink. I started out on Cuban rum, but after about the sixth saloon switched over to beer, which Howard Dietz had sagely been drinking from the beginning. After another half-a-dozen stops, I became the evening's first casualty and gratefully opted for the subway as my means of continuing the rest of the way home. Howard Dietz was the last man in the game that night, having—in what must surely border on being a supernatural feat—lasted all the way to 33rd Street before he passed out on Herald Square. Rum and beer is a hideous combination, and it wouldn't have mattered if I'd slept standing on my head that night. I was sick for two days and have been the most sparing of social drinkers ever since.

It was fortunate for me that alcohol lost most of its appeal then, as my schedule demanded a clear-eyed sense of concentration. In addition to my persistent attempts at trying to endear myself to most of Barnard's student body (as Captain Spaulding might have said—"And what bodies those Barnard students had!"), and continuing to make frequent contributions to F.P.A.'s column, I was also carrying a full academic load. I was also working for our campus newspaper, *The Spectator*, first as a reporter, and in my junior year, as a daily humorist penning "The Off Hour." Capping off my student career, I assumed editorship of *The Jester*, the school's monthly humor magazine, during my senior year. How I ever found the energy to cover all those bases is beyond me now, but as whirligig as my life was then, events were about to take place that would make it seem tranquil in comparison.

While still a senior, I turned twenty-one in October of
1916, which qualified me to vote in the presidential election in the following month. Woodrow Wilson was running for re-election, and I was very impressed with the
humanitarian legislation that he had fought for, which
included the eight-hour work day, child labor protection
laws, and the Clayton Anti-Trust Act which is considered
to be the Magna Carta of labor relations.

The dominant issue of the campaign, however, was
whether the United States should enter into The Great
War. Reports of the carnage taking place on the European battlefields had continuously fueled long and strident debates on the Columbia campus since the war's
outbreak in 1914. As the election drew to its fateful
conclusion, we were able to question or reinforce our
opinions from the theories being advocated by some of
the most respected leaders of the day.

Almost en masse, the School of Journalism would
frequently assemble at Madison Square Garden to sit
transfixed as Teddy Roosevelt vigorously championed
Republican challenger Charles Evans Hughes and his "cult
of preparedness," while William Jennings Bryant thun-
dered his eloquence on behalf of Wilson's pledge to
"keep us out of war." And while the Old Bull Moose had
been my childhood hero, I could not morally sanction his
call to arms. Even Winston Churchill was later to concede
that the only thing that four-year bloodbath accomplished
was to depose the Kaiser and the Czar—both of whom,
for all their staggering faults, took on the saintly attributes
of Gandhi, in comparison to their successors Hitler and
Stalin. Wilson received my first vote.

Because we were still years away from being blessed
with the advent of computer projections, instant analysis,
and Dan Rather, the election of 1916 was a cliffhanger. It
took two days to tabulate the returns that trickled in by
telegraph. Actually, this was considered quite an accomplishment in speed and accuracy, considering that Ari-
zona and New Mexico had achieved statehood, making a
total of forty-eight states that had to be tabulated.

Fearing that a Hughes election would precipitate the end of civilization as we knew it, the Columbia campus seemed to be collectively holding its breath during the agonizing interim. All hope expired for awhile, when in preview of the 1948 "DEWEY BEATS TRUMAN" snafu, the bulldog edition of several New York newspapers proclaimed Hughes as the winner. When word finally came to us that four thousand votes in California had put Wilson over the top, there was, as one exalted journalism student put it, "a sigh of relief across the campus which raised whitecaps on the Hudson."

The Wilson victory elation was very brief. The narrow margin of his victory made it very obvious to a great many of us on campus that the Sword of Damocles was suspended over America by a thread which unraveled another turn with each U-Boat attack.

In the months that followed the elections, Columbia transformed itself from an academic setting into an extended debating forum. Classroom attendance became very irregular as impromptu rallies and debates were constantly taking place in Funard Hall, the cafeteria, and on the steps of the library. When enough students would actually convene for a class, the professors could seldom confine us to the subject for more than a few minutes before the impassioned rhetoric broke out anew.

For my part, I wrote editorials against involvement and joined the Intercollegiate Socialist Society. I didn't believe in the feasibility of utopia gained through socialism anymore then than I do now, but they were highly organized, and I was convinced that passive acceptance of an impending evil was as great a wrong, if not a greater wrong, than the original act.

Having committed myself to what I believed to be a just cause, I frequently armed myself with anti-war pamphlets which I pressed into the hands of the bemused, indifferent, and annoyed (ranging from mild to fierce) pedestrians along Broadway between 96th and 116th Streets. I carefully avoided the northwest corner of 112th

Street which I conceded to a highly memorable barefoot, bearded, bedraggled, self-proclaimed prophet of doom dubbed the Columbia Cassandra, who could usually be found attempting to scream the world into preparing for the imminent resurrection of Genghis Khan and his Army of Destruction.

It was German U-boats and not Mongolian hordes that had us worried over the 1916 and 1917 Christmas and New Year holidays. In February, a flurry of attacks on American freighters off the coast of Ireland, followed by a decree from the Kaiser that the Imperial German Navy would sink without warning any ship found to be within an extensive zone outside the twelve mile limit, signalled the end.

Over the Lincoln's birthday weekend of that year, a small group of us from Columbia were given a unique opportunity which, in our soon-to-be-surrendered naivete was calculated to have an outside chance at averting the impending apocalypse.

George Sokolsky, Al Seadler, Jimmie Danahy, M. R. Werner, and myself had gone to the opening night performance of Elmer Rice's short-lived play *Iron Cross*. During the intermission, we met Henry Wadsworth Longfellow Dana, who was in charge of the comparative literature department at Columbia. He was very anxious about whether or not President Wilson was going to accept the German dare, and had organized a delegation of prominent New Yorkers that were leaving for Washington at midnight to make a direct appeal to the president in hopes of preserving our neutrality. Dr. Dana asked if we would like to join his expedition. We assured him that we would, but a quick examination of the exchequer produced less than ten dollars among us. Dr. Dana seemed amused by this and airily told us not to worry as Mrs. J. Sergeant Cram, a name I recognized as being one of the leading matrons of New York society, was underwriting the entire trip.

Having missed the second act of the play to return to

our respective homes and pack a bag, we reassembled at
Penn Station in time to meet the train. Dr. Dana introduced us to Mrs. Cram, who seemed somewhat disori-
ented by the whole affair. She nodded to us, and we
scrambled up the steps and squeezed into the pacifist-
crammed Pullman.

There was no sleeping that night; the talk and excitement was non-stop. Norman Thomas, who was then barely
into his thirties and already white-haired and avuncular,
seemed more or less to be the leader. I had admired his
speeches at Madison Square Garden, and that night we
struck up a friendship that was to last until his death in
1968.

Around dawn we arrived in Washington, too excited
to realize how tired we actually were. A fleet of taxis
caravanned us to a small hotel near the Capitol where
Mrs. Cram had taken over a floor. The five of us from
Columbia shared a small room, and after a mostly unsuc-
cessful attempt at freshening up, we joined the others in
the dining hall for a breakfast pep-talk.

After we had eaten, Dr. Dana gave us a list of senators
and representatives who we were to visit and poll as to
their stance on ending neutrality. First on our agenda was
Senator Luke Lee of Tennessee, who spoke with the sort
of mellifluous, rapid-fire intensity that one tends nowa-
days to associate with used car salesmen and television
evangelists. After the war, Senator Lee tried to capture
the Kaiser from Doorn where he had fled to write his
memoirs, which, to the dismay of a New York publishing
syndicate who bought them sight unseen for a million
dollars, turned out to be unbearably long and dull.

Senator Lee politely listened to our pleas and then
politely remarked, "Gentlemen, I don't agree with a single
statement you've made."

Our next notable was Senator Henry Cabot Lodge,
historical nemesis of Woodrow Wilson and the League of
Nations, whom we encountered unexpectedly on the steps
of the Capitol. Brusque in both manner and appearance,

accentuated by glaring eyes framed in black by his spiky beard and top hat, he could easily have passed for the vaudeville house stock villain who gets hissed as he forecloses on the mortgage and forces the defenseless ingenue and her blind grandfather to walk out into the snowy night. We barely had time to introduce ourselves before he walked away, leaving us with an over-the-shoulder snap about "being polite to one's elders."

It was to go that way for the rest of the afternoon, at the end of which we returned to the hotel tired and frustrated but buoyed by the thought of getting to present our case to the president the following morning.

Nearly one hundred of us marched into the White House the next day and were promptly escorted into the Green Room by the Secret Service. To our crushing disappointment, we were not met by the president, but by his secretary, Joseph Tumulty. Despite these circumstances, Norman Thomas was somehow or another able to give a spirited reading of our resolutions. When he had finished, Secretary Tumulty's gracious response about how the president regretted that the pressures of his duties prevented him from personally meeting with us, but would carefully review our proposals, was delivered with an open countenance that concealed his searing impatience with the entire proceedings. We unisoned a hollow "thank you" to the secretary and silently filed out of the White House, making our way through the anti-prohibition picketers, and crossed the street to the headquarters of the Women Suffragists who had prepared tea for us. That afternoon, we rode the train back to New York in a gloomy silence.

I recounted what I had seen in Washington in a series of *Spectator* articles that were well received by both students and faculty. I was grateful to be in an environment where reasoning still prevailed, but this too, was soon to be illusory. When we received news of the declaration of war on 6 April 1917, the campus underwent an instantaneous metamorphosis. War, which only the day before had been abhorrent in concept, now seemed to be embraced with the sort of pep-rally enthusiasm that one experiences on the eve of the homecoming football game. In retrospect, the students' behavior was understandable; that of the faculty, especially Dr. Nicholas Murray Butler, University President, was not.

Dr. Butler was unquestionably one of the greatest men in the history of education. He was associated with Columbia University for sixty years, for forty-four of those years, 1901 to 1945, as its president. During his tenure the schools of journalism, business, dentistry, social work, public health, library service, and education were established, elevating Columbia's status to that of one of the country's most renowned universities. He also served as a special presidential envoy to several administrations, persuaded Andrew Carnegie to establish the Carnegie Endowment for International Peace, of which he was the president for twenty years, and was the co-author of the Kellogg-Briand Peace Pact in 1928, for which he shared a Nobel Prize. This was a League of Nations referendum which outlawed war, and we can all applaud Dr. Butler for his efforts. Goodness knows what mischief Hitler might have gotten himself into had the Kellog-Briand Pact not been there to keep him in line.

Riding in tandem with Dr. Butler's altruistic bent, however, was an ego whose healthiness frequently exerted itself to such an extent that it was difficult to determine which force was pacing the other. His political ambitions were anything but a secret, and after serving in New York's delegation at several GOP conventions, he was picked by President Taft to be his running mate when Vice-President James Sherman died during the 1912 campaign. Having lost that election to Wilson, he wisely abstained from challenging the incumbent in 1916 to concentrate his efforts for the top spot in the 1920 race.

While a student, my contacts with Dr. Butler had been brief and somewhat strained, due in large part to an oft-quoted jibe—"Who is that dapper fellow in the sleek cutaway who may be seen crossing the campus every morning just before nine o'clock? That is not our president, that is our butler"—that had been attributed to me. (Guilty.) When I assumed editorship of the *Jester*, I paid the obligatory visit to his office, where he encouraged me to "Keep us laughing."

In my naivete, I had assumed that it was conviction and not political trend-spotting which had been responsible for the highly visible support that he had lent to preserving American neutrality. After the declaration, he issued a flurry of pro-war statements and communiqués that astonished the campus by their pulverizing tone of righteousness. It was a political pirouette, the likes of which I was not to see again until 1978, when Governor Jerry Brown of California was to jump the fence following the Proposition 13 mandate and embrace the issue with a fervor that paled the exuberance of its authors, Howard Jarvis and Paul Gann.

I had little stomach for the whole affair, and as we were preparing the May issue of the *Jester* at the time, I took the opportunity to satirize Dr. Butler's abdication of principles in a poetic editorial, "The Little Red School on the Hill." This was far from being the funniest or even the most incisive piece that I had written up to that time, but it contained one sentence in which I referred to Dr. Butler as "Czar Nicholas of Columbia," which was to make it one of the most consequential of my efforts.

The magazine returned from the printers and was distributed to the students on a Tuesday afternoon. On Wednesday I was backslapped and congratulated from one end of the campus to the other; on Thursday I was called into Dr. Williams' office.

Dr. Talcott Williams had postponed his retirement to become the first dean of Columbia's School of Journalism. He was engagingly eccentric due to a memory that was rapidly approaching the hoariness of his appearance. He was especially confounded in his ability to remember names by the fact that there were two students in the

Journalism School named Seadler, Al and Si. Employing one of the simplest problematic resolutions since Alexander the Great faced the Gordian Knot, Dr. Williams overcame his affliction by simply referring to every student on campus as "Mr. Seadler."

When I walked into his office, I sensed trouble was at hand when he greeted me by my right name. In a voice comprised of nervous fear marbled with a strong element of affecting grandfatherly concern, he told me that Dr. Butler was so enraged over my editorial that if I didn't seek to immediately make amends, I could very well find myself expelled from school. My first reaction was total disbelief. The acuteness of Dr. Williams' anguish dispelled this feeling, however, replacing it with a burning indignation. Taking my inspiration from Socrates and Sir Thomas More, I replied in a barely controlled voice that I had no intention of groveling to Dr. Butler or anyone else, and that in my opinion, it was Dr. Butler who should be doing the apologizing. Case stated, I turned and walked out. Severe perhaps, but you know how it is with us martyrs.

On Friday, rumor had it that the student council was going to be convened in a special session on Monday to ask for my resignation. The whole thing seemed too preposterous for me to give it any credence, and I was able to dismiss it from my mind over the weekend as I began preparing for the impending final exams.

Persephone danced over the weekend, and on Monday I returned to the campus in high spirits. The student council rumor proved to be true, and that afternoon I was summoned before them and indeed asked to resign. I refused, was thanked, and told that the matter would be given further consideration. The next morning the axe fell.

I was given the news by Dr. Williams in his office. I was later to learn that Dr. Butler had held him responsible for my actions, and that he had barely missed censure himself. Recounting my "fine record" and the "cruel irony" of being deprived of my diploma with only six weeks left to go brought him to the edge of tears. Seeing no profit to be gained by that sort of emotional scene, I thanked him for his example and counsel over the years and left.

Homeward bound along the Broadway, Dr. Williams' phrase "cruel irony" grated itself between phrases such as "freedom of speech" and "freedom of the press" in my mind, restructuring itself into "cruel injustice." I was in no sort of position financially to take any sort of legal recourse, and with no other options presenting themselves to me, I decided that the healthiest thing that I could do was to accept the situation as one of the "thousand natural shocks that flesh is heir to," and get on with my life.

My main concern as I neared home was the painful disappointment that I was about to cause my parents to undergo. Not only was I the first to be born in America, but I was the first member from either side of the family to reach the university level. Under those circumstances, it wasn't hard to understand why they seemed to take more pride and enjoyment from my accomplishments than I did.

As I always ate at school, my presence in the kitchen as my mother was preparing my father's lunch announced trouble. Sitting my mother at the table, I explained what had happened and told them how sorry I was that all of the sacrifices that they had made to finance my education had been in vain. My mother asked me if I thought that I had done the right thing. When I said "Yes," my parents shared a look of understanding for which I still bless their memories. Rising from the table, my mother said, "Then we don't worry about it anymore. Now, how do you want your eggs?"

Late that afternoon I returned to the *Jester* office to clean out my desk enroute to the Lion Saloon where my "shiva" was being held. It quickly turned into a crowded rollicking affair, and I was amazed and flattered by the turnout. Commiserating over an endless succession of mugs of nickel beer, reproachfully referred to by George Sokolsky as "workingman's gin," my friends, sterling characters that they were, rousingly demonstrated their empathy over my expulsion by getting the lot of us expelled from the Lion around 10 P.M. Assembled on the sidewalk, philosophically if not legally intoxicated from the effects of our camaraderie, Howard Dietz lifted a purloined mug to toast my future with, "May you forever be profound, prolific, and published." Bowing curtly, I turned and walked home, twenty-five blocks along Broadway—a nighttime excursion that I would strongly advise anyone not to make today.

I am loathe to think that any portion of my life could be governed by a jingoistic platitude, but the expression "My country—right or wrong" does contain a basic truth, that as an American, I feel safe in embracing. I thought then as I do now, that war is abhorrent. I had done all that I could to prevent America's involvement, but the freely elected representatives of the populace had determined otherwise. Responding from a sense of commitment and not contrition, and certainly with no delusions of military glory, I reported to the Naval Recruitment Center off Times Square the day after my expulsion and applied for a commission. Over the next few days I was subjected to a barrage of written and physical examinations, all of which I easily passed until I took my eye examination.

In his book, *Where's the Rest of Me?*, Ronnie (President Reagan) writes of how his military career hinged on passing a similar test. He fudged by squinting through a slit in the fingers of the hand which covered one eye while he pretended to be reading from his uncovered eye, and then reversing the process. It sounds like a neat trick, but even had I known of it, my eyes were too far gone, even at that stage of my life, for it to have done me any good.

When my turn came, I faced the chart with the rows of diminishing-sized letters and correctly read them. A second reading without my glasses was an embarrassment for all concerned. I was sent into another room where I was ordered to toe a line and remove my glasses. That done, an examiner pulled down a rolled-up chart which had the relief outlines of various types of ships illustrated on it. Without my glasses, the images of the ships painted black against the white chart fused together into a sort of blurry Rorschach test from which I derived an erotic image of an obese female accordion player I had once seen at the Palace, the further details of my perception I think best not to go into on these pages.

Blind as the Grey sisters when Perseus stole their eye, I proceeded on as gamely as I could, and in the process identified cruisers as destroyers, submarines as ocean liners, and the battleship *Maine* as the Staten Island Ferry. I was thanked and sent home to await further instructions. In a few days, an official government letter arrived which informed me that my military status had been reclassified, and that I needn't worry about serving until the War Department ran out of children and old people.

Spared from military service, I went to work while the rest of the country went to war. It had been my intention upon graduating to apply for a job as a reporter with the *World*. (The fact that the *World* was owned by the Pulitzer family who had endowed Columbia with the School of Journalism from which I had so recently been ejected somewhat complicated the issue.) Seeking counsel, I went to see Frank Adams, who put in a call to the *World*. Hanging up, he said, "Go see Swope, kid. He likes moxie."

Recently I answered some questions from a journalism student who astonished me with the fact that she had never heard of Herbert Bayard Swope. I suppose this only underscores the haunting reality of how fleeting fame can be, but in my salad days, Swope was the "icon" of journalism and the hope of working with him was my sole reason for wanting to sign on at the *World*.

Swope came to New York as a young man and secured a reporter's job on the *New York Herald* where he quickly proved to be both a blessing and a curse to his editors. He dazzled them with his ability to take a sheet of facts, study them for two or three minutes without making any notes, and then type up a ready-to-print, eight hundred-word article in less than fifteen minutes. He exasperated them with his chronic absences, one of the more famous of them being the time he parlayed a two-dollar loan into a $6,000 winning streak in a crap game and wasn't seen at the *Herald* for a month. After enduring several suspensions, he was finally fired.

Unemployment proved to be no problem for Swope. His motto was "Spend money as if you have it, and somehow, you always will." Joined by his roommate, John Barrymore, who had not yet taken to the stage but was working (even more erratically than Swope) as an editorial cartoonist for the *Evening Journal*, illustrating (of all things) the evils of alcohol, the two of them made an irresistible duo of society blades who cut an ingratiating swath into the eagerly receptive strata of Manhattan's monied set. They were wined, dined, housed, clothed, and bankrolled to such an extent that Swope was able to exist entirely on his social talents for two years before one of his benefactors secured him a job at the *World*.

As a reporter for the *World*, Swope quickly fell into his familiar routine of absenteeism and subsequent suspensions that would have surely resulted in his termination, had it not been for an incident in 1913 which culminated in opportunity coupling with ambition to whelp the Swope legend.

Since many of you are reading of Swope for the first time, I think it safe to assume that the details of the Rosenthal case are equally unfamiliar to you. Briefly recounted, they are: Lt. Charles Becker of New York's police force was appointed head of Special Squad Number One by Police Commissioner Rhinelander Waldo (the man that James Cagney came out of retirement to portray in the film *Ragtime*). Special Squad Number One was created to clean up New York's gambling and prostitution. Unable to rid the city of vice, Becker embraced the adage "if you can't beat them, join them," and in one year banked $100,000 on a $2,200 salary. There was a double-cross with a gambling house operator named Rosenthal whom Becker had had murdered by four hit men named Whitey Lewis, Lefty Louie, Dago Frank and Gyp the Blood (could a reporter ask for a better copy?), before Rosenthal could turn state's witness. Recognizing the story as the once-in-a-lifetime opportunity that it turned out to be, Swope latched onto it with the grip of Antaeus. Due to his extensive contacts all over the city, he was able to crack the case by tracking down a newsboy who had inadvertently witnessed the murder outside the Metropole Hotel and persuading him to testify.

It was a superior piece of investigative reporting that stunned New York, no stranger to city corruption, as layer upon layer of official malfeasance was discovered. After dozens of front page exclusives in the *World*, Swope became the toast of the city.

The story concluded in 1915, when Becker followed the four assassins to the electric chair at Sing Sing after being denied his mercy plea by newly elected Governor Charles Whitman, who had ridden into the governor's mansion on the crest of publicity that he garnered while prosecuting the case as Manhattan's district attorney.

Swope became the *World's* star reporter and was sent to Germany in 1916 as a war correspondent. He returned and published *Inside the German Republic*, a lengthy study of the Kaiser's war effort, which brought him the first Pulitzer Prize for reporting. Spiraling on a parabola of seemingly unlimited dimensions, Swope became the *World's* city editor in 1917 and was made managing editor in 1920.

Swope had been named as the *World's* city editor about two weeks prior to that memorable day when his secretary escorted me into his office for what surely must be one of the briefest job interviews on record. There was no exchange of amenities. He pointed to one of the chairs in front of his desk, and I sat down, placing my hat in the vacant seat. He studied me for a moment and leaned forward in his chair: "Are you sorry you wrote that article about Butler?" Since I hadn't apologized before, I saw no reason to start now. Imitating his gruffness, I reached for my hat and rose to leave. Before I could turn for the door, he cut me off with: "You might work out alright. You can start tomorrow." Years later, when the Broadway success of *The Cocoanuts* gained me entrance into one of his famed weekend parties on Long Island, he told me that the reason that he had hired me was because he didn't like Nicholas Murray Butler any better than I did.

The *World* building was located at Park Row and Frankfurt Street, a block from city hall. Built by Joseph Pulitzer as a monument to himself, it boasted stained glass windows facing the street on the lobby level, one of which is now on display in the Journalism Building at Columbia, and was topped by a gold dome that Herman Mankiewicz assiduously declared to be "gilded from within by the exhalations of Mr. Pulitzer."

The city room, where the art of expense account padding was perfected, was located on the twelfth floor. The room itself was noisy, crowded, and ventilated by windows that were invariably stuck—open in the winter, shut in the summer. It was there, at a desk beside the entrance to a memorably foul-smelling men's room, that I was to spend the first two-and-a-half years of my professional life.

I was the first reporter that Swope hired. Following me, Norman Krasna, Heywood Broun, Alexander Woollcott, Deems Taylor, Lawrence Stallings, Maxwell Anderson, Robert Benchley, Dudley Nichols, Herman Mankiewicz, Walter Lippmann, James M. Cain, George Hough, and Howard Dietz were either to launch or firmly establish their careers under Swope's aegis, making the *World's* city room one of the most distinguished matrixes in the history of the fourth estate.

Lawrence Stallings and Maxwell Anderson were to jump directly from the *World* into the literary limelight by writing *What Price Glory?* during a series of lunch hours, stolen hours, and after-hours sessions in the *World's* seldom used cafeteria. And Britton Hadden established another special niche in the Swope folklore immediately following his graduation from Harvard, by explaining to Swope that he wanted to gain a year of reportorial experience and then found his own publication. Swope had no openings at the time, but hired Hadden when the resolute youth brazenly declared, "You're interfering with my destiny." After a year's service, Hadden resigned, and shortly thereafter cofounded *Time Magazine* with Henry Luce, presumably also following the dictates of destiny.

It didn't take me long to realize that the life of a professional reporter bore little resemblance to the world of student journalism. Several stars matriculated through the *World's* city room, but by and large, the permanent staff of reporters were, as was the case with so many reporters of that era, a cynical, hard-drinking, shabbily-dressed lot whose graph lines on the insurance companies' actuarial charts seldom surpassed the forty-year mark.

A great deal of the disreputable status that reporters were forced to endure could be attributed to the size of our paychecks, which were grossly disproportionate to the effort that it took to earn them. We received a nominal salary, but derived most of our income from "space rates." Columns of print were measured in inches, so many dollars to the inch. This system produced a natural tendency toward wordiness, which was countermanded by a somewhat sadistic assistant editor who wielded his red pencil with the relish of a Samurai swordsman in full battle. At the end of the week, we could clip out our articles and present them to the cashier, who calibrated them into our take-home pay, such as it was.

Joseph Pulitzer had managed the *World* by impressing his dictum, "Accuracy, terseness, accuracy," on each of his reporters. Less pretentious, but certainly no less effective was Swope's standing order, "Pick out the best story that you can find and hammer the hell out of it." It was very good advice, but during my first year at the *World*, I had little chance to follow through with it. As the most junior reporter assigned to the city desk, I worked as a "legman." I would go out and cover a story and then return with my notes which would be turned over to a veteran reporter who would write the story for publication. On payday, the veteran reporter would inform the cashier as to what percentage of the story the legman had contributed, and we would be paid accordingly. Although the reporters maintained a rather cynical perspective on the general condition of mankind, they were always square with me when it came to space rates, and I never felt that I was cheated.

It was an exciting time to be a reporter in New York City: troops were either embarking to or returning from the war, there was an armistice to celebrate, cemeteries to dedicate, and the enactments of the eighteenth and nineteenth amendments, which gave women the right to vote and bootleggers an opportunity to get rich. I'll always be grateful for the experience, but after two-and-a-half years on the *World*, it became obvious to me that there were warning signs on the wall, or more precisely, at Percy's Hole-In-The-Wall Saloon, which was located on the lobby level of the *World* building. There were reporters like myself who would stop there occasionally after work, there were those who not only stopped there every night, but also spent all of their lunch hours there, and there were those who more or less lived there. With attendance in each of these groups bearing a direct ratio to the reporter's seniority, I decided that if it were impossible for one to make it through this vale of tears with one's poetic lights undimmed, one's spiritual petrification could at least be accomplished on a more comfortable level than would be possible on the puny salaries doled out by the Pulitzers.

Accordingly, I submitted my resignation in the early months of 1920. As I had no familial obligations weighing me down and a small bit of money saved up, I was able to act out the first stage of my adolescent fantasy of becoming a poet-playwright. I took a small apartment in Greenwich Village and began my attempt at setting the Hudson on fire.

The resulting work, *Unaccustomed As I Am*, which I dedicated to "The Great American Democracy, may it bring me royalty," was brought out by Knopf in 1921. Then as now, there is not much of a living to be made in verse, and my collection, which was released with little fanfare, probably would have sunk without a trace had it not been for my family and friends. But it was published, and the thrill of that accomplishment has not dimmed through the passing of these many years.

When my friends and relatives had bought their dutiful quota of the book to thereafter distribute as wedding, graduation, and bar mitzvah presents to what I would assume to be a host of disappointed recipients, the term starving artist became a reality to me.

With a bank account rapidly approaching zero, and with no prospect for its regeneration, I was sitting in my apartment desperately trying to figure out my next career move when opportunity, in the guise of a Western Union delivery boy, knocked on my door. To my supreme astonishment, he bore a telegram from film star Katharine MacDonald's producer whom he was informing me, had been impressed enough with my book to want me to come to California to write titles and continuity for her next picture. If $250 a week was acceptable, tickets and advance would follow.

The word thunderstruck would be entirely applicable here, but I did have the presence of mind—despite trembling hands—to write out a reply and tip the messenger with the last of my grocery money. I was to spend the rest of the day walking amidst the free spirits, revolutionaries, and fellow poets in Washington Square Park muttering to myself, "This can't be true, it just can't," but as this was normal behavior for that area, little notice was taken.

I knew nothing of the film business, and even less of California. As with all true New Yorkers, I tended to regard everything across the Hudson as the place where the natives raised our food and would let you take their pictures in exchange for some shiny beads and trinkets. The name California rang a bell from my schooldays, but I always confused it with "Remember the Alamo," Pike's Peak, and "I'll Take My Stand In Dixie." The names Hollywood and Beverly Hills seemed to have some association with it, but I couldn't remember if Beverly Hills was the capital of California, or California the capital of Hollywood. It was reputed to be either in or bordering on a desert, which was faintly reassuring to a person whose childhood had been filled with endless recountings of the exploits of his ancestors who had found their fame by wandering for forty years in one. Thus emboldened by my heritage, I boarded the 20th Century Limited a few days later in hopes of seeking my destiny, be it burning bush or golden calf.

CHAPTER THREE

In those steam-powered days of yore, the New York/ California transit meant enduring what the railroads were advertising as "a pleasant trip from sea to shining sea in just four days." Of late, there seems to be a great swell of nostalgia for the romance of train travel. Mostly, I suspect, from those too young to have known just how tortuous four days of jostling, sooty confinement on a train could be. Today, the same trip can be made in four hours, but the three-day bout of jet lag that accompanies it hasn't persuaded me that we've really gained anything. (" . . . When I was at home, I was in a better place: but travelers must be content.")

Due to the floodgate that was opened by the success of Cecil B. de Mille's production of *The Squaw Man*, Hollywood had only been "Hollywood" for less than ten years when I first encountered it. And with its mostly unpaved roads, ramshackle buildings, and rampant rate of inflation, the Hollywood of 1921 really did have the look and feel of a boom town. What it did not have, has never had, and will never have—the Southern California climate being an unsuitable host for its survival—is holly growing anywhere near its vicinage. The misnomer was merely the fanciful invention of Mrs. Daeida Wilcox, who adopted the bucolic appellation for her fig ranch in the 1880s. Contrived though the title might have been, Mrs.

Wilcox has my thanks for having chosen it. Had her literal-minded husband prevailed, I would have spent a goodly portion of my career working in Figwood, and what Muse would have been inspired by that?

It was Ben Schulberg who had summoned me to Hollywood. One of the founding giants of the film industry, and one of the most decent men that I ever knew, he was exemplary, a credit to his chosen profession. Unfortunately, the profession that he chose was one that is no stranger to frequent acts of cruelty. A few years after our association, he was to become the head of production at Paramount Pictures. And after guiding the studio through one of its most profitable periods, his reward was to be abruptly squeezed out of his job in a power play that was to leave him a spiritually broken man. There's an excellent account of that dismal episode in *What Makes Sammy Run?*—in my opinion, the best novel about Hollywood ever written. (*What Makes Sammy Run?* was written by Schulberg's son, Budd, and since there's such a laudatory reference to me in it, I've always wanted to repay the compliment.)

Before her early retirement, Katharine MacDonald was one of the great stars of silent films. With her statuesque looks, she became known as "The American Beauty," but she was too wise to waste her talents working for others. Taking her friend and frequent co-star, Douglas Fairbanks, as a mentor, she formed her own production company, and after a few hits (the tax laws of that time were certainly a suitable basis for nostalgia), Miss MacDonald was able to leave films as a wealthy woman.

The MacDonald-Schulberg partnership's first production was *Stranger Than Fiction*—a crime melodrama with a villain named "Black Heart." It had been filmed and edited, but they weren't happy about the title cards in the comic relief portion, and that's where I entered the story. I worked on the picture for about a week, everyone seemed pleased with my effort, and the day after I finished, I boarded the Super Chief for New York.

I had quite a few tempting factors to overcome before deciding to return to New York: Schulberg had offered me a very generous contract to stay and work on scenarios, and there was the temperate climate, the cornucopia of pretty girls that always seem to be associated with the movies, etc. But the one, and I guess the only reservation that I had about Hollywood at that time, was the type of writing that was required for silent films. One had to think solely in terms of visuals, and for comedies, that meant slapstick. I felt that I was best suited to a wordsmith, and with that thought–or at least, hope–I hied myself back to New York. Although the realization of that goal was to be quite a ways off, it certainly proved to be a judicious call. Silent films achieved quite a degree of artistic achievement, but when the changeover to sound was made, very few of the writers–and stars–were able to adapt themselves to the new medium.

Thanks to Ben Schulberg's recommendation, I was able to secure a position in the publicity department at Fox Pictures when I returned to New York. Since Schulberg was under no obligation to me, an almost perfect stranger, I was touched by his gesture. The salary certainly wasn't equal to what I was earning as a scenario writer, but it was quite a few cuts above what I would have earned as a newspaperman. And thus relieved of my dread at the prospect of becoming a reporter again, I joined the ranks of that curious species of modified Muchausens known as press agents.

William Fox was the most powerful magnate in Hollywood during the 1920s. Along with most of Hollywood's pioneering moguls, he was the product of the turn-of-the-century wave of European-Jewish immigrants who settled in New York. Rising from a child laborer in a garment district sweatshop, he bought a nickelodeon which prospered, which led to a chain of theaters, which led to a production company, which led to his mighty studio which was worth an estimated $200 million in 1928. He was bankrupted in the '29 crash, and forced to relinquish the

remnants of his mighty empire which merged with the
floundering 20th Century Pictures to form, phoenix-like,
the 20th Century-Fox organization that gave rise to the
Darryl Zanuck fame.

At the height of its power, though, Fox Pictures had
the greatest stable of stars in Hollywood and could boast
of releasing a new feature film every week. Those of us
who worked in the publicity department had quite a time
trying to keep up with that much output. And about all
I can say of the experience is that I stayed with it for two
years, and as a future fictioneer, I couldn't have had a
better training ground.

When Ben Schulberg returned to New York after
parting with Katharine MacDonald, I was happy to go
back on his payroll. He had set up his own production
company to showcase the talents of a beautiful little spit-
fire from Brooklyn named Clara Bow. He recognized her
as the star she was about to become, but he was uncertain
as to what would be the best way of building her fame. My
stint as a Fox publicist had wearied me of concocting
phony images, so that my contribution to Miss Bow's
career was the suggestion that she remain exactly as she
was, a working girl from the middle class whom nature
had seen fit to bless with the most electrifyingly sexy aura
since Little Eva went to the World's Fair.

The idea was accepted all around, and I began to set
up meetings with reporters. Our first luncheon was to be
with Louella Parsons, who wrote for the Hearst chain.
Miss Bow, enjoying the first tastes of success, wanted to
dine at the Ritz, but I insisted on a chow meinery. The
informality worked, and Miss Parsons gave her career a
big boost. About a dozen luncheons followed, and
Schulberg took his rising star back to Hollywood, where
he became head of Paramount Pictures and she became
the biggest star of the decade as the "It Girl."

Following the success of *Cocoanuts*, I was invited to
become a regular member of the legendary Algonquin
Round Table, but I declined to accept because of an

incident that had taken place there the preceding year. The Algonquin is located on 44th Street off Times Square. The food at that time wasn't particularly noteworthy, but the convenience of its location made it popular with people who worked in the area. One day I happened to be eating there with two friends of mine who were reporters for the *New York Times*, and who were, like myself, Jewish. As we were leaving, Frank Case, the image-conscious manager, pulled me aside and said, "I don't like to see more than two Jews sitting at one table."

I've had a lot of brickbats thrown at me in my time, but nothing had quite the sting to it that that one did. Because my two companions were reporters, it didn't take very long for the story to get around, and when George Kaufman heard it, he threatened to leave the Round Table. Not wishing to lose the star member of his hotel's star attraction, Case made a formal, public apology to me, which I accepted, but for some reason I've never had any desire to set foot in the Algonquin again.

I've never regretted having not accepted the Round Table's invitation. Their legendary reputation as humorists was certainly well deserved, and although several of their members were to become close friends, especially Kaufman and Marc Connelly, there was a large element of superciliousness in their humor, a great deal of which was directed at the customs and ideals of the inhabitants of Smalltown, U.S.A. I found it very unappealing. As most of the Round Table members were originally from Smalltown, U.S.A., their self-styled sophistication quite often seemed to me to smack of self destruction. At any rate, being free of the Round Table freed me for eligibility in what I regard as one of my best memories from the twenties, the Cheese Club.

As might be inferred from its title, the Cheese Club's membership were a rather cheesy lot. Emotional refugees from the realities of adulthood might be a better description, "smart-assed" might be better still. Over the years, our legacy was to be completely eclipsed by the Round

Table's, but during its short life span in the twenties, the Cheese Club's notoriety often surpassed that of the distinguished gathering at the Algonquin. This was mostly due to the fact that, as the Cheese Club was mainly composed of press agents, publicity tended to come rather easily to us.

The club was founded with no particular aims or objectives other than to create a fraternal setting where the press agents of the theater district could congregate to fulminate over the shared frustrations of their work. Officers were elected, but that was as close to any sort of formal organization as we were ever to attain. Since we never had an office, the lunch counter of the Hotel Hermitage at 42nd and Broadway served as our headquarters until we were run out by the management who hoped that our absence would attract a better class of customers. Thereafter the club became peripatetic, up and down Broadway, in and out of chow meineries, lunch stands, and beaneries, one step ahead of indolence, two steps behind respectability.

The spirited, oftentimes inspired, but ultimately undergraduate level of humorous antics displayed by a group of men releasing the safety valve on their mounting frustrations probably doesn't warrant a retelling on these pages. I mention them, though, because it was while I was a "cheeser" that the dream I had been nurturing since my childhood suddenly came within my grasp.

Every cent that I had earned since my errand-boy, grammar school days had come through writing. I had been a poet, reporter, motion picture scenarist, and press agent, with praiseworthy judgments accorded to me in each endeavor. What I could not do, however, was write a play. Sketches and lyrics yes, and a few of those found their way into some hit revues. But when it came to completing a full-length play, I was stopped cold. In retrospect my problem is easily recognizable. I was stopped by that most insurmountable of creative obstacles, "wanting it too badly."

During the summer of 1924, the Cheese Club had graciously volunteered its services to officiate at the Sunday swim meets in Luna Park where the girls from the Follies would challenge the girls from the other shows on Broadway. When the coming of fall brought the games to an end, the idea of putting on a show was proposed as a constructive channel for our wayward energies. The motion passed, and thereafter, every day at lunch, plot and dialogue suggestions were randomly shouted out and duly recorded on a mounting stack of paper napkins. To this day, I can't offer any explanation for the phenomenon, but during the gestation of the Cheese Club's play, the shroud of self-doubt and anxiety which had weighed me down into a creative paralysis suddenly seemed as lightweight and diaphanous as cellophane.

Word of our forthcoming "theatrical milestone" spread quickly, and the entire Broadway community got into the spirit of the joke. The great producer Sam Harris loaned us the use of his theater, but his manager insisted that we post a $4,000 bond to insure against any potential damage. With the Cheese Club never having more than $18 in its treasury, all of it in loose change collected in a wine carafe that sat on top of the dessert counter at Lindy's, this presented something of a problem. However, in the best traditions of the theatre, a check for the correct amount was presented to Mr. Harris' manager on the day of the performance, and the show went on. Thankfully, the manager didn't notice that the check was drawn on a bank in Shanghai which, even with the use of cable, took a week to clear.

The show was *One Helluva Night,* and it more or less lived up to its title. We were able to disarm all criticisms of our offering by labeling it as "the world's worst play, performed by the world's worst cast, in front of the world's worst scenery, singing the world's worst songs," the musical highlight of the evening being "I've Been Fired from Every Job I've Ever Had, That's Why I Fell in Love with You." The newspapers responded in turn by sending the "world's worst critics to write the world's worst reviews."

The performance was a sellout. Most of the cast and crew seemed to have had little regard for Mr. Volstead and his legislative masterwork, evidenced by the boisterous scene in the lobby where the veracity of the good-luck telegrams from such theatrical luminaries as O'Neill, O'Casey, Shaw, Shakespeare, and Sophocles was questioned.

When no one could think of any more good reasons for delaying the proceedings any longer, the conductor was summoned. The tone of the evening was set during the overture, when a man in the audience yelled out, "Tell that son of a b— playing the piccolo to keep in tempo"—which prompted the conductor to halt the orchestra and demand of the audience: "All right, who called that piccolo player a son of a b—?" This was retorted by, "Who called that son of a b— a piccolo player?"—which led to the orchestra walking out in a huff to be replaced by an organ grinder from the street corner.

Other high or lowlights of the show had the Equity cast going on strike during the first act and being replaced by their understudies (Cheesers), the scenery being confiscated for lack of payment during the second act, and the third act never materializing as the announcement in the program was explained away as a typographical error. A good time was had by all, even by those who actually paid to get in, and at the end of the show we were given a standing ovation. Almost every paper in the city had a critic there that night, and the next day, we were the toast of the town. Sam Harris offered us a contract to take the show through the rest of the season, but the idea of success, not to mention the possibility of having to actually show up every night, frightened us into leaving it as a memorable one night stand.

As had been feared, success ultimately proved to be the undoing of the Cheese Club. When all of the expenditures from *One Helluva Night* had been met, the Cheese Club, to its simultaneous horror and delight, found itself to be in possession of a $1,750 profit (considered to be a sizable sum by the standards of the time). It was in the disposal of this new found wealth that the Cheesers, like the protagonists of a Greek tragedy, brought about our own self destruction.

It all began with a discussion about the power of publicity. The discussion was centered around—and this is not an unpopular topic with press agents—how so many people in the public eye had been placed there through the unheralded efforts of their publicists. It was at the point that one uncharacteristically reserved Cheeser had an inspiration with a delicious potential to it. "You fellows know what publicity has done," he said, "and I know, but suppose we prove it." Having always prided myself in the ability to recognize a cue, I burst in with, "How?" It is so often a terrible obstacle, that word "how," but the inspiration of the hitherto somnolent, suddenly animated Cheeser hurdled it with Olympian facility. "Let's take some totally unknown youngster," he said, "who has some talent but no opportunity. We'll use the money in the treasury to pay for her training, and then we'll get her in a show and put all of our publicity efforts together to put her over the top. And, granting some ability on her part, we should be able to make this Miss Nobody from Nowhere a national figure."

They applied—at first a few dozen applicants from the New York area, but as paper after paper across the country picked up on the story, applications from every state of the Union and every state of the society began coming in by the hundreds, the thousands, and then in a totally unexpected, mind-boggling avalanche of letters that required a convoy of postal trucks to deliver to the office that we were forced to rent.

Now offhand, the surprising situation that we found ourselves in, opening letters from and getting the addresses and telephone numbers of thousands upon thousands of young women who were eager to go on the stage, would seem to have an undeniably sybaritic allure

to it. But I wish to tell you that the only way I would ever
do it again is if Clint Eastwood were coming at me with
a gun in each hand. I'd take my chances with one gun.

There had been some mention of the phrase, "power
of publicity." But there's another phrase newspapermen
know, "pitiless publicity." And that, I am afraid, was—
unwittingly, of course—what our publicity stunt was—pitiless. For it seems to me now that it was altogether pitiless
to have raised the hopes we raised in the hearts of all
those girls when only one could win. It's a good thing to
have the fairy godmother suddenly appear and ask you
your heart's desire; it's another for her to tell you that
she's sorry, but someone else will be going to the ball in
the magic pumpkin that night.

In the main, the dreams of all those girls were silly
and stupid. But a silly and stupid dream may also be a
heartbreaking one. Come to think of it, that's the only
kind that is. Nobody, to my knowledge, has ever died of
a dream come true.

In the first place, to a surprising extent, the photographs submitted were those of homely girls, and beauty
is one of the stage's demands. There are some notable
exceptions, but ninety-nine times out of a hundred, you,
dear public, prefer a handsome heroine. Yet all of those
girls, photographic evidence to the contrary notwithstand-
ing, assured us they were "fairly good-looking." There is
something downright tragic about the ugly duckling's
calling the mirror a liar. She sees herself, surely as all girls
must, as a Princess Charming, but the committee could
only look on her with impersonal eyes. We didn't demand great beauty, but we did want appeal. So few of the
contestants had it.

In the second place, and I'm not sure but that this
comes even before the first place, an amazing number of
contestants submitted no photographs at all. And it wasn't
that they didn't understand the rules. They wrote, frankly,
that they couldn't afford it. And one pictured them, silk-
stockinged and a little hungry, run-down heels under slim

ankles, dreaming somehow in all their work-a-day woes the dream of electric lights on Broadway. We weren't a sentimental committee by any means, but had it been possible, all of them would have been given auditions.

The entries seemed to break down into three categories. Those in the lighter vein could be represented by the following: "My appearance is so different from the people around me they whisper, 'She's an actress.' I walk 10 or 12 miles every day with a big dog, and have for it received a marvelously perfect body, a dancing walk, and radiate the joy of a perfect health."

It was a little harder laughing at those in the second group, such as: "I have read about your contest and am very much interested. Am fifty-one years old and employed as a dressmaker, but have always wanted to play the piano, and am sure I could if you would help me. Please help me, dear Cheese Club, to realize my ambition and I will always be grateful to you."

The third category was made up of those who were totally without humor. Hauntingly memorable from this group was the plaint of a girl who wanted to know: "Would an unhappy married girl with a child be eligible?" Our contest was her last ray of hope. If we could take care of her child while she was studying, she would repay us every cent. It was sad to note that our contest attracted more letters of this type than any other.

Oh, there were bright bits too, but behind them all was tragedy, if you only looked. Women obviously in their forties wrote that they were twenty-five. One gallant old soul whose photograph indicated that she was fat and fifty admitted being thirty-five. "I weight 190," she wrote, "but I could easily take off 15 pounds if you thought it was necessary." We thanked her just the same.

To arrive at some sort of manageable figure, the committee was callously forced to adhere to the rules, and all entries that were not accompanied by a photograph were callously discarded. Even so, this left us with a roomful of applications that took us months to cull through until we had narrowed the list down to around two hundred hopefuls. Another month was spent conducting the intense auditions that produced one radiant winner and one exhausted Cheese Club.

The youngster that we ultimately chose was one of the loveliest looking ladies that these ancient eyes have ever seen. Additionally, she had been blessed with a fine voice and the gracefulness of a natural dancer. Casting agents were brought around to watch her singing and dancing lessons, and in a very short time, she had offers from both Broadway and Hollywood. Stardom seemed assured for her, and with it would rise the prestige of all the underpaid, overworked, unappreciated, two-fingered-typing publicists in show business.

Unfortunately, we had hung our hopes on a star that would never shine. The trajectory of Miss Nobody's stardom was stopped by the widening girth of impending motherhood and a rush to the altar. Crestfallen, we slinked back to our jobs, and Mrs. Somebody, née Miss Nobody, slipped from the limelight, taking with her all of our enthusiasm for continuing with the Cheese Club. For my own part, I was glad to be done with it, as all of my time and energy were soon to be focused on the deadly serious business of writing comedy.

CHAPTER FOUR

One afternoon in the summer of 1925, I found myself, much like the character in the Robert Frost poem, taking the road less traveled, and it did indeed make all the difference. Actually, I should say street instead of road, because the turning point in my life took place in Times Square.

After leaving my office at 42nd Street and Broadway, I was walking uptown with Tony's as my destination. This was a West Side restaurant that was popular with writers, reporters, and the flotsam and jetsam of the Cheese Club. And although the path to Tony's was usually well-beaten, business at that time was slow due to a poisoned shipment of beer. Remember that in 1925 the nation was collectively going through a phase of temporary insanity known as the Prohibition, the result of which was to enrich bootleggers, quite often at the peril of the consumers. Like most speakeasies, the patrons of Tony's were periodically subject to mild cases of ptomaine poisoning. This particular shipment, hastily brewed in an abandoned paint factory in Weehauken, proved to be totally unfit for human consumption due to some dead rats that were found floating in the barrels. The management at Tony's, enterprising fellows that they were, made the most of a bad situation by arranging for the police to raid the premises. Having thus fulfilled their quota for the season, they were insured that when a good shipment did arrive, business could proceed as usual. Supposedly it even worked out well for the taxpayers. The word had it that when the rotgut was poured down the sewers, they ran more freely than they had in years, but me thinks that this is a bit on the apocryphal side.

On that fateful day I was twenty-nine-years-old, still single, and earning a comfortable living working—somewhat restlessly—in the publicity department of Paramount Pictures' New York office. Having spent what I felt to be a very successful morning writing a campaign that was a sure-fire bet to convince moviegoers that their lives would be irrevocably incomplete if they didn't pony up a quarter to see the next Rudolph Valentino picture, I decided to get away from the stifling heat of the office and reward myself with a long leisurely lunch at Tony's. Normally I would just go across the street to the Metropole, but in the dank, subterranean storage rooms at Tony's I knew that I would find not only a respite from the city's annual summer swelter but probably a card game as well.

Despite the heat, the walk to Tony's was a pleasant one. It took me through the heart of the Theater District, and in my heart of hearts, that's where I wanted to be more than any other place on earth. And yet, while I was there, I still wasn't part of it, and this tended to make me feel as if I were on the outside looking in at the world's greatest party. Thanks to George S. Kaufman, the door to that party was about to open for me.

At that time, George, who was seven years older than I, had already written thirteen Broadway shows, most of them hits; several of them were even then considered to be classics. With the sharpness of his satire, George had revolutionized theatrical comedy, and so successfully had he staked out this area, that his name was being measured. He was amazingly inventive, constantly sought after by producers, and much to my surprise, walking toward me on that broiling afternoon when I was headed for Tony's.

I had maintained a casual acquaintanceship with George that dated back to 1919, when Frank Adams' first annual dinner for the "Conning Tower" contributors made our social circles concentric. But other than those yearly dinners, our relationship was limited to chance encounters, usually as we were entering or leaving a restaurant. It would have been presumptuous of me to have referred to him as my friend, as I was flattered that he remembered my name. You might well imagine, then, how I felt when this highly celebrated man of the theater informed me that he and Irving Berlin (whose standing in the theatrical community was also of a rather high order) were working on *The Cocoanuts* for Sam Harris. It was to star the Marx Brothers, and he would like me to collaborate with him on the book. Some men, it seems, are born great, some men achieve greatness, and some stumble into it blindly in front of Child's at 43rd and Broadway.

I never did ask George why he chose me to collaborate with him. At the time, it would have been a case of looking a gift horse in the mouth; later, when I was established, it didn't seem to matter. Until our encounter on the street, I hadn't received any communication from him about the project, so it may well have been that I was simply at the right place at the right time. However, it should be mentioned that I co-wrote seven more projects with George over the course of the next ten years, and in that time I never once saw him act on impulse. In both his life and his work, he was maddeningly meticulous about matters that most people would consider trivial. At this point, the answer is academic and lies buried with George. Whatever his motivation, whether he chose for one moment in his life to be cavalier, or our encounter in the street saved him a phone call, the important point, at least from my perspective, was that it gave me a start, and the next morning at 10 A.M. I did just that.

At the beginning of our first session, George outlined a scene that was giving him trouble. It turned on a malapropism, or more correctly, a Chicoism, and he wanted to know if I had any idea on how it might be fixed. Anxious to dazzle with my ability, I sat down at the typewriter and gave what finally became known as the "Viaduct" scene my best effort. I finished and proudly handed it to America's premier comic playwright for approval. He looked at it for a few seconds, muttered angrily that it was all wrong, and threw it on the table in disgust. Not daring to move or breathe, I sat there numbly trying to envision the total tonnage of crow that Paramount would require me to eat in exchange for the job from which I had abruptly resigned the day before. When my heart finally left my throat, I asked him what specific objections he had with my writing. He said that the scene looked all right, but my typing was lousy. I looked at the page for possible errors, and finding none, asked him what he meant. In a voice that was just short of shouting, he said, "Look at how much space you're wasting with these margins." A quick comparison with a page he had typed revealed that I was indeed guilty of indenting an extra two spaces from what he considered to be an acceptable margin. The fact that George's standards didn't always adhere to what is known as common practice was, as far as George was concerned, an error on the part of the world, and not him.

He was, simultaneously, the wittiest and the most basically unhappy person that I have ever known. He was a compulsive writer who took little enjoyment from his success, other than that it allowed him the opportunity to write yet another play. He was generous with handouts to anyone on the bad side of his luck, but would search through his incoming mail for uncancelled stamps that he could steam off and reuse. He could be a gracious host in his own home but a merciless persecutor of waiters in restaurants. Once, after a particularly embarrassing scene caused by a waiter bringing me the wrong order, I asked him why he regarded them with such ire. He replied that with the relative simplicity of their station in life, there was no reason why they shouldn't be perfectionists.

Like a number of America's celebrated eccentrics, George had a self-generated phobia of germs. He washed his hands on an average of fifteen times a day and would go to great lengths to avoid any sort of physical contact with another person, such as a handshake or a kiss. This aversion also applied to objects that, although they were not seemingly potential germ transmitters, were potentially messy and therefore were regarded as abhorrent and not to be touched, such as carbon paper which, in those days, was the principal means of paper duplication.

In all of the projects that we worked together, George would never allow carbon paper to be used. And because of this, a second copy was never made until the finished work was sent out to a typing service. In my days as a reporter, I had interviewed Edgar Lee Masters, who told me about the time that he had left his only copy of *Spoon River Anthology* on the seat of a taxi, and of the torturous ordeal that he went through during the rewrite. The prospect of a careless cleaning lady putting George and myself in a similar position permeated my dreams every night that we worked on *The Cocoanuts*.

Writing *The Cocoanuts* was quite a challenge in that we had to somehow write a full-length play with as little plot as possible. Having seen the Marx Brothers in their Broadway debut *I'll Say She Is* the year before, it was clear to us that any sort of structured complexity would work against the show. It was the non-stop assaults of the Marx Brothers that audiences responded to, and when they were offstage the audience would be distracted by either trying to replay in their minds what the boys had just done, or anticipating their reappearance. This affected Irving Berlin's score to an even greater extent than it did our book. And because of this, *The Cocoanuts* was the only major production of Irving's career that didn't produce a hit song, although we could have had "Always," one of the most beautiful numbers that that extraordinary man ever wrote. But George, who looked on romantic sentimentality in much the same way that children respond to castor oil, dropped it from the show.

The storyline that George had conceived had Groucho as Henry W. Schlemmer, Chico as Willie the Wop (my apologies to the Italian Anti-Defamation League, I changed it when I wrote the movie version), Harpo was Silent Sam, and Zeppo was a continuing problem.

There just wasn't any way to squeeze another comedic personality into an act that already had Groucho, Harpo, and Chico. Zeppo couldn't sing or dance or play a musical instrument, and although he was the best looking of the brothers he still fell short of matinee-idol status. So with all those avenues closed to him, there wasn't anything left for him except to play the straight man. George and I tried our best to invent some business that would more fully incorporate him into the act, but we were being pressed for a late fall opening which stopped us cold. The best we could do for Zeppo was give him the thankless role of a hotel clerk. It was the smallest role he ever played with the team, but he accepted the role without a complaint. A few years later, he finally did call it quits, which was a wise move. He set himself up as an agent and in that endeavor he became far more respected than he ever could have as a performer. The studio ayatollahs whom he was always out-maneuvering certainly respected him. And as one of his clients on whose behalf he played executive hardball, he certainly had no trouble eliciting mine either.

I can't really say that I came to look on the Marxs as the brothers that I never had—the wayward cousins that I never had perhaps, but not the brothers. But starting with *The Cocoanuts* I was to be more involved with their careers than anyone else. I saw them at their lowest, and I saw them at their best. What was unique about my perspective was that it let me see how different they were from each other.

Take Zeppo, for instance. While he might have been one comedian too many on stage, off stage he was by far the wittiest of the brothers. This would have given him a valid reason for brooding about his fate, but until he had made his break from the act, he deferred to the best interests of the group. But that would never have been true of Harpo and Chico, who demanded that every one of each other's musical solos be matched by one of his own. And as for their personalities being different, the best that I can do is employ the term polar extremes and apologize for its inadequacy, because Chico was unlike any other person that I have ever known. Quite a legend has grown up around Chico's amorous exploits, but all that I choose to say on the matter is that the legend, at best, has only been half told, and in the name of decorum it should remain that way. Harpo on the other hand was very sweet and shy around girls. He swore that he would never get married, and it was a vow that he kept for an awfully long time. And when he did take the plunge, it was a vow that he kept for the rest of his life.

And then there was the Grouchmeister. Throughout all the years of our friendship, I was forced to accept a lot of ribbing from Groucho because of my height and my education. Drawing himself up to his full 5'8", Groucho was able to tower over me by a quarter of a foot. It was seldom that he got to do this over another man, so that until the vicissitudes of seniority reduced us to the same level, I was doomed to being addressed as "Shorty."

Because Groucho had spent his early years on the vaudeville circuits, he was denied the opportunity to pass through the mill of higher education. This made him respectful of anyone who had, or who at least had tried to better himself intellectually. Of course he expressed his respect for me in typical Groucho fashion by zinging me at every opportunity. If I gave him some dialogue that he liked, I was rewarded with "Not bad, Shorty, for a college boy." Dialogue that he didn't like was dismissed with, "Shorty, for this you went to an Ivy League school?" It wasn't hard to detect the envy in his barbs, and when he finally did lower his defenses, we entered into a best-friend relationship that was to last for fifty-two years.

With Groucho, being best friends meant more than is

usually implied by the word. It meant entering into his world. Soon after I met him, I found myself going to his doctor, his lawyer, his dentist, his tailor, and most importantly by Groucho's lights, his stock broker. Until that time, I had resisted the investment fever of the twenties partly from lack of funds, but mainly from lack of understanding. Trying to make sense of the stock market pages in the newspapers was as incomprehensible to me as Egyptian hieroglyphics. Groucho assured me that if I invested, his broker would do all of the work, and that my only concern would be spending the profits. When it was put in that perspective, it seemed like a very civilized arrangement. But apparently my father's Old World values were more deeply ingrained in me than I would have thought possible, and for some time I continued to resist Groucho's urgings.

When I finally did become a risk capitalist, it was due to impulse buying, and thereby hangs a risky tale. It all began one fine spring day during the run of *The Cocoanuts* when Groucho invited me to his club for lunch and a round of golf. We had just reached the sixth tee when Chico came wheezing and gasping down the fairway to tell Groucho about a hot tip that he had just received on Canadian Marconi preferred. Groucho was normally a careful man about investments, but a tip is a tip, and Chico's enthusiasm was infectious. "I'll buy a thousand shares in the morning," he promised. But Chico said the stock would go up at least ten points by morning and urged immediate purchase. It was 2:35 and Groucho still had twenty-five minutes to become a millionaire, whereupon Groucho pulled me off the course, golf shoes and all, into his car, and the three of us whizzed into his broker's office at 2:57. Groucho breathlessly ordered a thousand shares, and, by 2:59:30, he had persuaded me to join the wealthy by buying a hundred shares.

At 10:00 the next morning I was in a broker's office studying the strange symbols that would enable me to retire at an early age. As it happened, the first announcement that flashed over the Dow-Jones news service gave Canadian Marconi a prominent mention. By order of the board of governors, it had been stricken from the board and all trading in it suspended. Most of the other stocks waited for the big crash that came in '29, but this baby didn't fool around.

Having been stung so early in the game, I wisely abstained from any further stock ventures by putting my money into bonds. Of course when the crash came, these were the first to fall. But until that fateful day in 1929 when Groucho and I sat in the investor's room of the Astoria Hotel and watched our fortunes fall with the speed of a thunderbolt from Olympus, I had the smug satisfaction of knowing that I would never be a victim of anything like Canadian Marconi again. Groucho lost the $250,000 that he had accumulated over the previous twenty years. My loss was considerably smaller, but no less painful, perhaps even more so, since I was to be married in December of that year. But with nothing to be gained by morose retrospection, we all kept going. And in December of 1929, with Groucho as my best man, I got married.

I would be remiss if my memories of the Marx brothers didn't include a mention about Margaret Dumont, whose association with the boys also began with *The Cocoanuts*. By self-design, as it turned out, she was a great and dignified lady. Although not born to wealth or social status, she had adopted a patrician perspective which she was convinced best suited her personality. In fact, so successfully had she sloughed off her former identity that I was amazed to learn that she had spent most of her life as a showgirl using the name Daisy Dumont.

I was fascinated by her from the moment we met. She would often come to me during the rehearsals of our various shows and ask me to explain what a particular line of a dialogue meant. I would spell it out for her and then marvel at how anyone could fail to understand what was so obvious—and that a great deal of the Marx Brothers material was very obvious is a point that doesn't need to be belabored.

Whether Maggie's naivete was an act, I still can't say. I strongly suspect that she was convinced that great ladies weren't expected to have great intellects, and she responded accordingly. I base this judgment on several decades of observing the theater world. No one could have been a showgirl for as many years as she was without acquiring at least a modicum of street savvy. If my theory is correct, then she should be lauded for the longest running performance in show business history, for she never slipped from her character until her death forty years later.

Nevertheless, it became obvious from the very first rehearsal of *The Cocoanuts* that the addition of Miss Dumont to the act filled a long-neglected void, and that a great comedy team had been launched. The boys especially relished their scenes with her, because now they weren't dealing with an actress who was merely playing a stuffy matron, but with the genuine article.

Once we had absorbed the nuances of our cast, the actual writing of *The Cocoanuts* went smoothly, and George and I were able to complete the script in about six weeks. But when we went into rehearsals, the script was to become the basis for a lot of friction between George and the boys. They had promised—indeed George only agreed to work on the show after they had promised—not to fall back on their old habits of straying from the text. And it wasn't that they didn't respect George or the script, quite the contrary, but sticking to a routine just wasn't in their nature. So, little by little, our lines began to be altered by Grouchoisms and Chicoisms and even Harpoisms—all of which were met by some very stinging Kaufmanisms.

The rift continued between George and the boys during rehearsals and came to a head when we were having the out-of-town tryouts in Boston. George and I had stayed up all night rewriting a scene, finishing just before the rehearsal that had been scheduled for 10 A.M.

The Marx Brothers, being the Marx Brothers, were no-where to be found at 10 A.M.. When they still hadn't made an appearance by noon, George, with his no-nonsense demeanor frayed even further by a long, hard night with-out any sleep, blew his top and started to walk out. I knew that if *The Cocoanuts* were to close George would get another show, and the Marx Brothers would get another show, but the one person who had a good chance of not getting another show was me. Determined not to be the odd man out, I grabbed (the hour cometh, the man cometh) George by his coat lapels and held him there until he cooled off enough to see the situation by my point of view. When the boys arrived about an hour later, George chewed them out royally. They apologized and promised to behave and, most importantly, to respect the script as it was written. And again, they kept their prom-ise—until the show opened on Broadway.

I think it safe to say that the premiere of *The Cocoa-nuts* at the Lyric Theater on 8 December 1925 marked not only the beginning of a hit show, but a turning point in the art of comedy as well. The outreaches of that show are still very much with us today, certainly in the works of Woody Allen, and I dare say that comedians in genera-tions yet to come will continue to mine the same vein that was opened up by George Kaufman's effect on the Marx Brothers.

I was offered a co-credit as author on the *The Cocoa-nuts* book, but I declined to accept out of principle. Even though I had collaborated on about three-quarters of what became the final draft, I hadn't been a part of the story's conception, and thus felt that morally I couldn't claim the script as mine. It was an issue that I felt very strongly about, and in retrospect my stance served me well throughout my career. Later, in Hollywood, a pro-ducer threatened to sue me if I didn't put my name on a script that I was called in to rewrite. He felt that if word got around that I had taken my name off the credits, it would appear as if I were trying to disassociate myself from the project, and this might generate some bad press. But I held to my position, and the picture did well, so the whole matter was forgotten.

George Kaufman was surprised when I didn't take the credit for *The Cocoanuts*. I'm afraid that I put George in a somewhat awkward position, as it was widely known to what extent I had worked on the script, but when I explained my feelings to him, he was respectful of them. Being the generous man that he was, he sought to help my career along by insisting that when he cleared himself of his commitments, he would make a full collaboration with men on another project. I was elated at this, but as George always had five or six projects in various stages of development, that promise wasn't to be realized for another two years.

While waiting to work with George again, I filled in the interim years by writing revues. The first one, *Americana*, was originally to have been produced by Florenz Ziegfeld and Richard Herndon. Ziegfeld was going to provide the financial backing, and Herndon was to have supervised the production that J. P. McAvoy and I were hired to write.

The prospect of working for Ziegfeld was exciting, as his revues were the most lavishly produced shows on Broadway. Regretfully, that excitement was never to surpass the prospective stage due to a dispute centering around Ziegfeld's insistence that two buffaloes be included in the show.

Ziegfeld had a somewhat perverse regard for animals as performers, which led to his owning one of the largest private zoos in the country. He was always incorporating dog, parrot, and bear acts into his shows, and when he purchased the two aforementioned bovines from a circus that was in default, he was sure that we could "work up some funny stuff for them." This was not the sort of show that McAvoy, Herndon, and I had discussed with him. We had some very definite ideas about doing a topical satire, but Ziegfeld was insistent that a sketch with the buffaloes wouldn't alter the show's thematic tone. We disagreed, and in the ensuing discussions, Ziegfeld's intransigence led to his withdrawal from the production.

Herndon believed that we had the nucleus of a good show. He promised that if we would stay with it, that he would finance the project himself. It was a promise that he kept, but in doing so, he certainly proved that he was in no danger of being mistaken for Ziegfeld. The budget that he provided fell—and I'm being generous here—into the "shoestring" category, and it was on that that we proceeded. Henry Souvaine was brought in to write the music, but since there were no funds made available for hiring a lyricist, that job fell on me because, as Herndon put it: "You're a poet, aren't you, so what's the difference?" The difference is substantial, or we would all be walking around whistling the sonnets, but the point was lost on the penurious Mr. Herndon.

At that time, I was spending quite a few of my evenings up in Harlem. I didn't care much for the glitzy places like the Club Hot Cha or the fabled Cotton Club, but at some of the smaller clubs, especially the Yeah Man, the first generation of blues singers was introducing a new art form to the world. Caught up in the spirit of that movement, I wrote two songs for *Americana*, "Why Do You Roll Those Eyes the Way You Do?" and "The Nobody Loves Me Blues." And to everybody's surprise, especially mine, they turned out to be hits.

Throughout all of the rehearsals and the out-of-town tryouts in Atlantic City, those two songs had been the weakest spot in the show. When we returned to New York, our lead singer dropped out of the show over a financial dispute with our tight-pursed producer. At that point I was fed up with Herndon and ready to walk myself and would have, had it not been for one of those miraculous sort of events so indigenous to show business.

With less than a week to go before our opening, Helen Morgan was brought in to take over as our lead singer. I had never heard of her before, but it only took one rehearsal to make it obvious that New York was about to be hers for the taking.

Our producer was equally taken with Miss Morgan's talent, but not to the extent that he loosened his purse strings. Arguing that talent was the only thing that really mattered in a show, he had purchased, at a rock-bottom price, some of the most ridiculously garish looking scenery that I had ever seen. It had a lot to do with our original singer leaving the show, and Miss Morgan found it equally offensive—so offensive that she opted to go down in the orchestra pit and sing her numbers while seated on top of an upright piano rather than perform up on the stage. And while none of us that were involved in the show wanted to admit it, that sense of intimacy that resulted from that cafe-like setting went a long way toward substantiating Herndon's assertion. I mean, even if there had been a background supplied by Ziegfeld and staged by de Mille, it would have been inconsequential, because all attention was focused on Miss Morgan every time her incomparable voice sailed into

> Why do they always treat me like I was dirt? I got the lonesome misery. Down in my heart I got the hurtin'est hurt—Oh, the Lord, he throws the awfullest woes on me. I got those Nobody—wants—me, Nobody—likes—me Nobody—wants—me Blues.

After *Americana*, Howard Dietz and I consummated a long standing wish by collaborating on *Merry-Go-Round*. Henry Souvaine wrote the music, and Richard Herndon used the profits that he had made on *Americana* to give us a first-class production (this being a stipulation that Souvaine and I insisted upon before agreeing to do the show). A few of the songs that we wrote for the show, "Hogan's Alley," "Sentimental Silly," and "If Love Should Come to Me," turned out very nice. And the songs plus the impressive production budget helped to make *Merry-Go-Round* even more successful than *Americana* had been. Thanks to the show's success and the rewards that it offered to a footloose young man in the world's greatest city, I felt that I was on the brink of my career break-

through, and the imminent attainment of that goal occupied my thoughts to such an extent that I was too restless
to enjoy the fruits of my labor.

The show that I did enjoy writing, the show that I had
wanted to write all my life, finally did become a reality
when the Marx Brothers concluded their two-year tour
with *The Cocoanuts* and returned to New York the summer of 1928. Sam Harris was anxious to bring us all
together again, and George Kaufman and I were only too
happy (well, at least I was) to oblige him by writing *Animal Crackers*. We followed the formula that George had
devised for *The Cocoanuts*, five large comedy scenes
(George referred to them as block scenes) strung together by the musical numbers. Two very fine gentlemen,
Bert Kalmar and Harry Ruby, wrote some very fine songs
for the show, but with the exception of "Hooray for
Captain Spaulding," which became Groucho's theme song,
their score suffered the same fate as did the one that
Irving Berlin wrote for *The Cocoanuts*.

On the first day that I worked with him on *The Cocoanuts*, George established one rule: if either of us came up
with a line that the other didn't like, that line will be
omitted on the theory that half of the audience wouldn't
like it either. This is a rule that I would recommend for
all theatrical collaborators. At that time, however, it was
a rule that I couldn't force myself to obey. It wasn't that
often that one of George's lines gave me pause, but when
it did happen, how was a neophyte like me supposed to
tell *the* George S. Kaufman, "Nah"?

With *Animal Crackers*, though, I was—and George certainly went to great lengths to make me feel so—an equal
partner, and as such, I had no qualms about challenging
him. Again, there weren't that many times when the need
arose, but when it did, he wasn't the least bit hesitant
about relegating any of his materials to the wastebasket.

Over the years I've received more mail about *Animal
Crackers* than any other project I was associated with. And
invariably the question is asked, "Which of those lines did

Kaufman write, and which are yours?" Having written forty-two of his forty-five plays with a partner, George was also frequently asked that question. His standard response was that in a collaboration, ideas get batted back and forth so many times that it would be impossible to assign any sort of proprietary authorship. This has always struck me as the perfect answer: generous, fair, and accurate. Unfortunately it has never satisfied anyone, but it is the perfect answer nonetheless, and with exception of that line which I'm reclaiming to entitle this opus, I will offer no further amendments to George's assertion.

As great as their movies were, and I'm especially proud of the ones I worked on, I still maintain that the Marx Brothers were at their absolute best during the Broadway run of *Animal Crackers*. They never played any of their scenes the same way twice, and very few of their performances failed to top the one that preceded it. Thanks to the boys' self assurance, *Animal Crackers* turned out to be one of the biggest hits of the 1928-29 season. The show ran for over a year, at the end of which the Marx Brothers, feeling that they had given the stage the best that they had to give, left it in favor of Hollywood. I was invited to go to Hollywood with them, but since *Animal Crackers* was only my first Broadway credit, I elected to remain in the theater. I felt that my best was yet to come.

CHAPTER FIVE

Between his involvement on *The Cocoanuts* and *Animal Crackers*, George Kaufman had another go at writing a play without a partner. The result was *Strike Up the Band*, and in my opinion it was the play which came the closest to revealing George's true character. It was topical, uncompromising, devastatingly satiric, and unlike any musical comedy that had come before it. Unfortunately, what had made *Strike Up the Band* such a theatrical departure proved to be its undoing: it was too topical, too uncompromising, too devastatingly satirical, and especially, too unlike any musical comedy that had come before it. The critics raved about it, but in 1927 the public was enjoying the Coolidge prosperity and was in no mood to have their musicals remind them of the dark connection of wars and profits. Consequently the production folded in Philadelphia during the second week of its pre-Broadway run.

Strike Up the Band was produced by Edgar Selwyn. Along with Ben Schulberg, he had been one of the founders of Hollywood. And like Ben Schulberg, Edgar's thanks was to be on the receiving end of one of the industry's earliest corporate squeeze-outs. Edgar landed on his feet back in New York, and after a few successes there, namely *Strike Up the Band*, he was able to get back in the Hollywood game.

Edgar had a tremendous admiration for what George had written. He had also lost a great deal of money when the first production closed, and that's when I became involved. In the fall of 1929, Edgar thought that the mood of the country had changed enough to make another production a feasible idea. George concurred, but he had a tremendous aversion toward working on the same material twice. While he was working on the original version, George asked me to come over one afternoon and help him with one of the ingenue's love scenes (Another one of George's great aversions.). I made some suggestions that he was able to use, and on the basis of that familiarity, George thought that I should be the one to have a go at the revised version.

My familiarity with the Marx Brothers also worked in my favor as I ended up having to turn the show into a vehicle for Clark and McCullough. Here again I'm probably dealing in names that will be known only to those of us with a thick covering of moss on our backs. But in their prime, Bobby Clark (who used painted eyeglasses as a trademark the way Groucho did with a moustache) and Paul McCullough were as big on the vaudeville circuits as Burns and Allen, Gallagher and Shean (Shean being an uncle to the Marx Brothers), and the Marx Brothers themselves—albeit minus two brothers—and that similarity certainly worked in my favor.

The Gershwins were a team, I feel safe in assuming, that will stand on their own without any identification from me, but for the benefit of those who have been vacationing on Mars since Lindbergh flew the Atlantic, the Gershwins that I'm referring to were that brilliant musical cyclone, George, and his equally brilliant although far less cyclonic brother, Ira. For me, it was their music, far more than anyone else's, that made the New York of that time such a vibrant city, and we can all be grateful to Edgar Selwyn for having the foresight to match their genius with that of George Kaufman's in *Strike Up the Band*.

My association with the Gershwins extended back to Townshend Harris Hall when Ira succeeded me as editor of the school paper. And through Ira I met George, who attended a public high school for a year or two before dropping out. Later Ira and I were both in the Cheese Club, and when I was working on *Americana*, they more or less rescued the show for us by coming up with a couple of wonderful songs. One of them, titled rather prophetically, was "That Lost Barbership Chord." It parodied the barbershop quartets which supposedly died out at the turn of the century but were then showing ominous signs of returning to popularity. George and Ira's song became quite a hit, but I've never heard it played since *Americana*.

The music from *Strike Up the Band* is still very much with us and remains special to me, as that show was the first time that I was privileged to be a full collaborator with the brothers Gershwin. What I especially remember from our sessions together is being amazed at the telepathy that existed between them. I've never seen anything even remotely like it with other songwriters, certainly not with the composers that I've worked with. Having watched Ira merely nod to get George to play one section from a particular melody from one of a dozen songs in front of him, or when George would play a few bars and exclaim, "It fits," before Ira would read the lyric that he was still writing—which did indeed fit—I feel secure in my belief that the genius of their songs was truly the product of one mind.

In addition to the brilliance of the Gershwin music, what made it particularly noteworthy was the graceful way that it could be used to advance a story. In light of all the shows that have opened since the twenties, it's probably hard for anyone who wasn't around then to understand what a stop-and-sing sort of an affair musical comedy was in its formative years. With their integrated scores, George and Ira changed all of that, probably more so than any other words-and-music team, and *Strike Up the Band* by far represented their best effort at that time.

In conjunction with my reworking of the script, George and Ira made a number of changes in their score. One of the most regrettable, yet necessary, was the deletion of "The Man I Love." That song—probably the greatest torch number ever written—had quite a checkered history. They had originally written it for *Lady Be Good* with the Astaires. Although it was a magnificent song, it didn't suit the mood of the show. But because it was such a magnificent song, they were able to use it to raise backing—and then find an appropriate reason to delete it—for three subsequent shows. "The Man I Love" did stay in the first production of *Strike Up the Band*, and afterwards you couldn't turn on the radio without hearing Helen Morgan belting it out, and by the time we did our production it was so well known it had to be dropped once again.

For our production the Gershwins replaced "The Man I Love" with the equally touching "Soon." They also resurrected "I've Got a Crush on You" from *Treasure Girl* which hadn't fared very well the year before. After World War II, Lee Wiley slowed that song down and popularized it as a sort of whimsical ballad. But in its original form, it was very up-tempo and served as well as a dance number.

The entire score of *Strike Up the Band* was a musical treasure lode, but my favorite of all of those great numbers was the title song. Ira redid part of his original lyric for the second production, but couldn't get the opening verse done to his satisfaction.

About a week before rehearsals were scheduled to begin, I went up to the townhouse that George and Ira were sharing on Riverside Drive. When I walked into their top-floor work area, George was seated at the piano and Ira was sitting at his desk mulling over that first verse. George played it through once and while he was doing so, the idea popped into my head. As he was playing it again, I took out a pencil which pretty much seemed to take off on its own. Both Ira and George liked my verse enough to leave it in, and thusly am I represented in the Gershwin oeuvre:

We fought in 1917
Rum-ta-ta-tum-tum-tum
And drove the tyrant from the scene
Rum-ta-ta-tum-tum-tum
We're in a bigger, better war
For your patriotic pastime.
We don't know what we're fighting for
But we didn't know the last time.

The song "Strike Up the Band" served as the finale to a first act in which tycoon Horace J. Fletcher of the American Cheese Company maneuvered Col. Holmes (Woodrow Wilson's trouble shooter Col. House served nicely as a role model) into forcing Switzerland to go to war after the Swiss protested against the 50 percent tariff on Swiss cheese. Although the world has distanced itself from the First World War by an additional two years at that point, one reading of the Kaufman script made me question whether the world was ready for a musical with that much bite to it—especially the part in the second act where the soldiers return home to find their jobs gone. The trick was to make it palatable without losing the bite, and I'm afraid that I failed in my effort. The show did become a hit, but the bite, of necessity, was one of wobbly dentures.

The necessity was that infamous egg that Wall Street laid. I had tried to redo the script and remain as faithful to George's original version as I could, but when the market crashed, Edgar insisted on drastic changes being made. The solution that presented itself to me was to have most of the story take place in one of the Fletcher character's dreams, with him awakening from it a la Scrooge—horrified by his previous war profiteering. This pretty much changed the show's emphasis from satire to straight-out comedy. Edgar was pleased with the results, and as investment money (including Edgar's) had for the most part dried up altogether, I could appreciate his reasoning.

There was, however, a scene in the original version in which Col. Holmes takes the liberty of declaring war so

as not to disturb the president's sleep. I wanted to incorporate that scene into the revised version as it would have
gone a long way toward retaining the spirit of what George
had created. For that reason, Edgar insisted that it be
dropped. We went around and around about that scene,
all the way through the rehearsals, the Boston tryouts,
and the Broadway previews, but the scene stayed out.

George Kaufman came to see the show on the night
after we opened. The reviews in that day's papers were
unanimously positive, and that fact wasn't lost on George,
who had suffered a tremendous paper loss in the crash.
Nor was it lost on Edgar who—as might be expected of a
man who had a hit instead of bankruptcy on his hands—
was ebullient. Just before the performance was to begin,
Edgar came up the aisle to where George and I were
standing at the back of the theater. I was telling George
about some of the changes I had made when Edgar interrupted with: "Morrie, are you still brooding about that
scene?" Edgar looked around at the sellout crowd for a
moment and chortled: "What difference could it have
made anyway?"

Had Edgar not asked that question, I seriously doubt
that George—who was basically apolitical—would have
taken any more ventures into political satire. Because he
was a man who expressed very few emotions, George said
nothing at the time, but I sensed, correctly as events were
to prove, that a challenge had been issued which George
had accepted.

George and I watched the show for about an hour,
and then went over to a coffee shop in Times Square for
sandwiches. He was quiet, almost distracted, while we ate,
but as soon as the waiter had taken away our plates,
George grew very serious. He said that we should do
another show together. He didn't know how or when it
could be done, but this one would be the way that we
wanted it done even if we had to put it up with our own
money. That put *Of Thee I Sing* into motion, and I'll
always be grateful to Edgar Selwyn for taking out that

Col. Holmes scene—which should have been left in the show.

When we finally got to the point of putting words to paper, it only took seventeen days to write *Of Thee I Sing*. Getting to that point, however, took a year and a half. In the interim, George wrote at least half-a-dozen shows, several of them simultaneously, including *Once in a Lifetime* in which he also acted (quite well), giving eight performances a week for several months. It was a schedule that would have done in a lesser man, and I still marvel at his ability to maintain it. He would often work with me in the morning, work with Howard Dietz or Alexander Woolcott or Edna Ferber in the afternoon, and then perform in his show at night. He never wanted to stop for a minute, and with his innate anxiety heightened by the crash, it was better that he didn't.

During that long period when George and I were having our planning sessions, not one word was committed to paper. Whenever one of us had an idea he would go to the other's apartment and talk it through. For the first few months this didn't really get us anywhere, but two important decisions were eventually made: the show would be a musical with the Gershwins as collaborators, and with the 1932 election drawing closer, it would be about presidential politics. With those two factors established, *Tweedledee* began to take shape. The concept was to show that the two major political parties, with the exception of their campaign songs, were as alike as Tweedledee and Tweedledum. We laid out an entire story using the opposing songs as our plot device, and the more we got into it, the better George liked it. But once we were really into it, I started to have some strong reservations about where we were headed.

There are those who will contest this, but politicians are people. And in order to get the audience involved in the show, we were going to have to play up the human side—the love interest as it is called. George bristled at this (the phrase "damned romantics" comes to mind). It meant throwing out three months' work, but with Ira's help, I was able to get George to accept what should have been obvious to all of us from the beginning. George retaliated by insisting that if there had to be a love interest, then the entire show would be about love, and thus was the "Wintergreen for President" campaign—with its platform of love—begun.

It took us about two months to come up with our new storyline, and this one was committed to paper. Using our outline, Ira then wrote the lyrics which we used as the basis for our dialogue. This was a reversal of the usual musical comedy evolution, but it brought the book and score together in a way that had all of us convinced—and this was a feeling that started on the very first day of rehearsal—something very special was about to happen.

With the exception of Porgy 'n Bess, which belongs in a class by itself, the Gershwins regarded the score for *Of Thee I Sing*—"Wintergreen for President," "Love Is Sweeping the Country," "Who Cares?," and that deliciously whimsical title song as their best effort. To this I would hastily concur and add that "Of Thee I Sing, Baby" is my favorite of all their creations, and with Lennore Gershwin's permission I would like to grace these pages with its reprint:

> Of thee I sing, baby
> Summer, autumn, winter, spring, baby
> You're my silver lining,
> You're my sky of blue
> There's a love of light shining,
> All because of you.
> Of thee I sing, baby,
> You have got that certain thing, baby—
> Shining star and inspiration,
> Worthy of a mighty nation,
> Of thee I sing!

With that one line—"Of thee I sing, baby"—Ira left quite a mark on New York. For years and years after the show closed you could hear construction workers chorus-

ing it down to pretty girls on the street, Yankee fans using
it to cheer Babe Ruth's homers into the stands, and
maitre d's coaxing corks out of champagne bottles with
it. The person who didn't want anything to do with it was
George Kaufman. To George, it seemed undignified. This
produced the only serious row in the whole production,
but with the Gershwins and myself outvoting George, the
song stayed in the show.

The success of a show ultimately depends on the
performers winning over the audience, and with William
Gaxton as the rakish John P. Wintergreen and Victor
Moore as the fumbling-bumbling Vice President Alexander
Throttlebottom, we had the best Broadway had to offer.
They had never worked together before *Of Thee I Sing*,
but their pairing proved to be Broadway's answer to
Hope and Crosby. In this regard, you have to hand it to
Hollywood. Those "Road" pictures will be around for-
ever, but the six Gaxton/Moore productions now exist
only in the memories of those of us who were privileged
to see them.

It was through the Throttlebottom character that
George and I were able to leave our mark on national
politics. There were some, mainly holders of the vice-
president's office, who thought we were being disrespectful of the second highest officer in the land. This was not
our intention, but we couldn't help ourselves when it
came to spoofing what was all too obvious. After all, the
vice president is the only person who is a member of both
the executive and legislative branches of government,
and there have been far too many times when a tragedy
has necessitated his taking over the mantle of power.
With that kind of power invested in the VP's office, it's
pretty sobering to review some of the people who have
been brought in to fill the position and the way they were
virtually abandoned after being inaugurated. Vic Moore's
perfect lampooning touched a nerve that helped—somewhat at least—to change that. Starting with John Nance
Garner in 1932, every VP for the next thirty years—

including Richard Nixon—came into the office vowing that he would not be a Throttlebottom. Not many of them succeeded, but at least the problem was given a name.

Having seen Vic in two previous Gershwin shows, *Oh Kay* and *Funny Face*, George and I modeled the Throttlebottom character after him. We weren't sure if we could get Vic for the part, but we knew that we at least wanted a Victor Moore type for our man. We had used our grand strutting mayor, Jimmy Walker, as the inspiration for the Wintergreen part, but we didn't have any particular actor in mind when we were writing the show. Sam Harris suggested Bill Gaxton, whom we hadn't known; a meeting was arranged, and our problem was solved.

Oftentimes finding the right person to play a supporting role can be more difficult than casting the leads. After seeing scores of actors for the role of Jenkins the White House press secretary, we were flummoxed. Once again Sam saved the day by bringing in a young hoofer named George Murphy. It wasn't a very large part, but in the right hands a little can go a long way, as George proved by stopping the show every night in the "Love Is Sweeping the Country" number. George and I were to become involved in quite a few adventures over the years, but I regret *Of Thee I Sing* was to be the only one in a show business venue.

Bringing the right people together was one of Sam Harris' greatest talents as a producer. An even greater one was his ability to leave those people alone while the show was being put into shape. Although he seldom came to rehearsals, Sam always knew exactly where the production stood. Once we spent all of an afternoon and all the following morning trying to block out a Throttlebottom scene that wouldn't allow itself to be resolved. After we came back from lunch, Sam came down to the set and asked if he could offer a suggestion. George shot me an eyes-rolled-back look of exasperation. He was not one to suffer fools lightly, but this was Sam, so he patiently listened to Sam's suggestion, and then patiently explained why it wouldn't work. Sam apologized for taking up our time and left. We returned to the scene, but after three hours of frustration, we were no further along than we were the day before.

Just as we were about to break for the day—and if this had been a cartoon, a light bulb would have appeared over our heads—we realized, without even trying it, that Sam's suggestion would solve the problem that had us stymied. It did indeed work, but we were never able to get Sam to acknowledge having even the slightest connection with making it possible.

Other than that one glitch with the Throttlebottom scene, we encountered very few problems during rehearsals, so few, in fact, that we became apprehensive about what was in store for us. As the director, George Kaufman was especially concerned. The memories of *Once in a Lifetime* were still very much on his mind, and if you've ever read Moss Hart's account of the prolonged struggle they endured while putting that show on its feet, you can probably understand his uneasiness about going from one extreme to the other. Shows—especially one which was attempting to blend music and political satire in a way that had never been attempted before—just don't click together that easily. We knew we had the makings of a hit, but at the same time we were never able to shed ourselves of the feeling that we had somehow taken a shortcut that was inexorably leading us to disaster. That feeling was to stay with us until the night of the Boston tryouts. After that, we had to accept the fact that we had reshaped the mold by capturing lightning in it.

We opened *Of Thee I Sing* at the Music Box Theatre on 26 December 1931, and for the next year-and-a-half it was "the" show in New York. The fact was to have a neutralizing effect on the rest of my career. The highs were never to reach that heightened sense of exultation again, and with the memory of *Sing* serving as a sort of emotional trump card, the lows could never hurt in a way that they would have otherwise.

Aside from the satisfaction of having proven myself in a city whose standards meant more to me than any other city on the planet, the success of the show provided a few other rewards. My cut of the gate, for instance. And in addition to my share of the royalties, I was also an investor—with a large "I"—everything I had and everything I could borrow. Everything I had and everything I could borrow didn't amount to any great sum, but what there was of it came back many times over.

And then there was that reward, the one that none of us had foreseen.

After I had spent most of the following spring working on the auditions and rehearsals for our national touring company, my wife thought I needed a vacation. I agreed, but I wasn't enthusiastic about the notion of a vacation that involved taking a trip. Whenever I had some free time, I liked to rise late, read the papers all the way through, go to the races or a ball game, see a show in the evening and catch the midnight show at a club. With New York offering that kind of variety, I've never understood why anyone would want to knock himself out taking a trip somewhere only to return home more exhausted than when he began.

My wife, however, occasionally felt the tugging of her country roots which required a communion with nature beyond that which could be found in Central Park. Now, there is a theory that travel broadens the mind, but in my case, traveling only proves that you can take the Jew out of Manhattan but you can't take Manhattan out of the Jew. We went, and I was fairly miserable the entire time, but for the sake of my lovely wife, I tried to comport myself in Spartan silence. What made this particular trip so displeasurable was the tension that arose between myself and our host/driver (his car) who had a mania about observing precise departure times that would have shamed Mussolini. Being a man of business, he wanted to get rolling in the early morning. Being a man of the theatre, I wanted to ease into the day in the early afternoon. We compromised, with much grousing, on mid-morning.

It eventuated, on our third day out, that I arose and repaired to the water closet (as the British would say) for my ablutions. While I was trying to solve a double acrostic that I had brought along, I heard Il Duce in the other room calling my name. Before I had a chance to answer, he burst right into the bathroom and shoved a day-old copy of the *New York Herald Tribune* into my face. And thus, in that position so common to us all, did I learn that George Kaufman, Ira Gershwin, and yours truly had been awarded the Pulitzer Prize for writing *Of Thee I Sing*.

A word about awards: Competition belongs on an athletic field. In the arts, to place a comedy in contention with a drama, and then judge one of them as "best," is just plain stupid. After moving to Hollywood, I was nominated for two Academy Awards. Zeppo wanted me to take out advertisements and be interviewed on radio shows—this was the standard procedure of those campaigns—but I wanted nothing to do with the whole business, nor did I attend the ceremonies. We were in the midst of trying to found the Screen Writers Guild at the time, and having a devil of time doing so. We needed all the help that we could get, and the Oscars, which, for my money are just one step short of the Miss America pageant, seemed like one more wedge being driven into our shaky coalition.

The Oscars have spawned the Emmys, Peabodys, Tonys, Grammys, and a host of other dog-and-pony extravaganzas that I don't know well enough to refer to by their pet names. (And such is their proliferation, that I expect an announcement will be made soon to trumpet an awards show to salute the best awards show.) I am told that the purpose of these shows is to generate the revenues which in turn support their respective academies. We can be thankful, at least, that they're not government supported enterprises, but may I suggest that if each film studio or television network or record company were to donate one-tenth of one percent of the profits from their biggest hits each year to those respective academies, the

same ends would be served in a manner far less specious
than the one which is currently used.

As awards go, the Pulitzer committee is to be thanked
for not subjecting their recipients to the nominating/
balloting process. But while the hoopla is absent from the
Pulitzers, their basic premise of "best" is the same as all
the other awards. I hadn't much enthusiasm about the
award for that reason, and because of George Gershwin's
exclusion, all of us were seriously tempted to refuse an
acceptance. *Sing* just wouldn't have been *Sing* without
George's majestic contribution, but the Pulitzer tenets
had no proviso for music, only the written word was to be
considered. But as the Pulitzer committee had never
chosen a musical comedy before, and there were a number of editorials charging that a serious mistake had been
made (such was the state of musical comedy then, and
perhaps still), we felt obliged to accept.

Were I the sort of person who gives in to baser urges,
I could give you another reason for accepting the Pulitzer.
You see, the Pulitzer Committee is an adjunct of Columbia University, and although he doesn't vote on the
committee's choices, the president of the university is
also the ceremonial head of the Pulitzers. And as the fates
would have it, Columbia's president in 1932 was, still, Dr.
Nicholas Murray Butler.

Yes, even today, I could still take a great deal of
satisfaction out of remembering that the man who had
thrown me out of his university was unable to make eye
contact with me when circumstances forced him to award
me that university's highest honor. But to do so would
smack of a most ungentlemanly form of gloating, so I
won't.

Vendettas aside, the awards dinner stands out in my
memory as a very pleasant affair. I had the opportunity to
meet Pearl Buck who was being honored for *The Good
Earth*, and General John J. Pershing, the MacArthur/
Eisenhower of that era who was being honored for his
memoirs, *My Experiences in the World War*. (And we thought
we had title trouble.)

But what was especially memorable about receiving the Pulitzer was the way it seemed to divide my theatrical career. *Animal Crackers, Strike Up the Band* and *Of Thee I Sing* had been solid hits, but I can make no such claims about my next three efforts.

However, I did have one victory of sorts before the flops began. Shortly after *Of Thee I Sing* was awarded the Pulitzer, a young man named Walter Lowenfels slapped a one million dollar plagiarism suit on everyone—with the exception of the cast, stagehands and ushers—who was involved in the production: Kaufman, myself, the Gershwins, their music publishing company, Sam Harris and Irving Berlin who co-owned the Music Box Theater, Alfred A. Knopf who published the play in book form, and George Jean Nathan who wrote a foreword for the Knopf book.

The basis of the Lowenfels allegation was that George and I had based our story, and Ira had based his lyrics on Lowenfels' unproduced play, *U.S.A. with Music.* That was patently untrue. None of us had ever read the script or heard of Mr. Lowenfels before his suit was filed against us. Ira and I were outraged by the charge, but George Kaufman took it all matter-of-factly. This was his third or fourth go-round with a plagiarism action, and there were a couple more of them waiting for him down the road. All of them proved to be totally groundless, but it seemed to have little effect in discouraging each of the successive parasites who tried to leech onto him.

Our desire to have the Lowenfels case tried on its merits ran into a snag. Because Mr. Lowenfels hadn't enough money to post a bond which would cover our legal fees in the event that he lost, a trial couldn't be scheduled. Not wanting to spend the rest of our lives with Mr. Lowenfels claiming that we had cheated him, and that the judicial system aided us because he was financially disadvantaged, we waived our right to a posted bond. Judge John M. Wolsey heard Mr. Lowenfels' arguments and promptly threw the case out of court for having no merit whatsoever. It was a very sorry affair, and with the legal fees, a very expensive sorry affair, and from what I've recently read about the Bee Gees—whoever they may be—this especially loathsome form of sorriness and its expensive resolvement is still with us.

Now, about those flops. It seems that every silver lining has its clouds, so I guess that I shouldn't be overly crabby about the little bit of rain that fell on my parade. Actually, looking on the positive side, I learned a lot from those experiences. On my first venture, *Pardon My English*, I learned how invaluable a producer like Sam Harris was to a production. This was a musical I wrote with the Gershwins and Herb Fields, whom I'd known at Columbia. Herb had a very impressive string of Broadway successes including, later, *Annie Get Your Gun*. Between us, I thought we had a pretty fair notion of how to write a show. The producing team of Aarons and Freedly (who had an equally impressive string of hits) had other notions. They changed almost everything we wrote, and the ensuing tug of war resulted in a total fiasco, best left forgotten, which it was after forty-six performances (save for the music).

George Kaufman and I spent about six weeks knocking ideas around for our next production, and when nothing would jell together, George's wife—the wonderful Beatrice—solved our problem by suggesting that we get back together with the Gershwins, Sam Harris, Bill Gaxton, and Vic Moore and do a show about Wintergreen and Throttlebottom running for re-election. The result was *Let 'Em Eat Cake*, and from this effort I learned that that terrible malady of show business known as sequelitis can be overcome by bold and imaginative writing.

Take, for example, Mr. Robert Garland, who was one of our finest drama critics. Oh, how well do I remember Mr. Garland's review of *Of Thee I Sing*. It was a joyously exuberant piece of writing, and one that I admired very much. Kaufman admired it. Sam Harris admired it. The

Gershwins admired it. Not only did we admire it, but we showed it to our friends. We praised it so often that the Pulitzer committee heard about the review, sent for a back copy of the *World-Telegram*, read it, and awarded the prize on the basis of its enthusiasm.

When it was announced that Mr. Garland, defying precedent, would write a review of *Let 'Em Eat Cake* as a sequel to his review of *Of Thee I Sing*, the wiseacres sneered and advised him not to do it. He could not, they asserted, hope to recapture that first, careless rapture. That was to be expected. There are always people who have loved your first child so much that they are ready and eager to hate the little stranger who comes to take its place.

But in all fairness to Kaufman, Harris, the Gershwins, and myself, we were not of that breed. We looked forward eagerly to the review, reserving our *World-Telegrams* months in advance.

Well, we read the sequel, and it is my unsavory task to report our findings. We just couldn't understand what had happened to Garland. Maybe the Pulitzer prize went to his head, or perhaps, our ravings about his first review so swept him off his feet he felt he could do no wrong. Whatever the truth, the fact remains that his review of *Let 'Em Eat Cake* was a feeble imitation, not to be mentioned in the same breath as its predecessor. And yet, I say that a sequel can be successful. You should have seen what Percy Hammond of the *Times* did with the same materials and the same cast. Now that was a review. But unfortunately, Broadway operates on a correlative of Gresham's Law which led to *Let 'Em Eat Cake* joining *Pardon My English* in the Great White Way's graveyard after ninety performances.

The final installment of my flop trilogy taught me the importance of having a good title, or more correctly, how dangerous it can be to have a misleading one. We titled it *Bring On the Girls*. Our problem was that we didn't. After *The Cocoanuts, Animal Crackers, Strike Up the Band, Of Thee I Sing*, and *Let 'Em Eat Cake*, it would seem logical to expect a show with the names Kaufman and Ryskind on it to feature a singing star with an acre or two of spangled chorines highkicking behind him. But at that point in his life, George, who had never liked musicals to begin with, was sick of them. He argued that a good writer was one who could carry a show from beginning to end without having to please the audience every twelve minutes with an up-tempo song. I didn't buy that theory. I think—I know—that there are far more challenges facing a writer who has to blend the book and the music into a fluid story, but I had never done a straight play at that time, and I thought it might make a nice change of pace. We went to great lengths to publicize the fact that the show was not a musical and that the title was a play on words, but it was to have little effect on our oh-so-restless audience.

Another reason for that show's failure might have had something to do with the fact that our second act was a real stinkeroo. The first act was probably the best piece of writing that we ever put to paper, but like countless playwrights before and since, we couldn't sustain it for the stretch. Had the circumstances been different, we would have put it down for a while and (hopefully) come back with a new perspective. But since the plot of the show revolved around the Reconstruction Finance Act— how many people today even know what that was? not many, I should think—and as events were moving so quickly, we had to get the show mounted before it became outdated.

We previewed the show in Washington in hopes that audience response would tell us how to go about fixing that unfixable second act. At intermission on our opening night, a scout from MGM stopped me in the aisle and offered to buy the film rights. I was trying to get backstage to give the actors some new lines that I had just thought up, but when the show ended, the scout, and a goodly part of the audience, was gone. We worked on that second act continuously for two weeks, and if anything, it only got worse. When it became obvious that it just wasn't going to work, we threw in the towel. Mighty good first act though.

We had written *Bring On the Girls* with Gaxton and Moore in mind, but Cole Porter already had them starring in *Anything Goes*, one of the biggest hits of the decade. In their stead we procured the services of Porter Hall in the Vic Moore role, and Jack Benny played the part that Bill Gaxton would have taken. While *Bring On the Girls* didn't take us very far professionally, it marked the beginning of a friendship between Jack and myself. A few years later, I made up for our first misadventure by writing *Man About Town*, which turned out to be one of Jack's most successful pictures and one of my happiest experiences in Hollywood.

Now I must ask you to please pardon the melodramatic tone of this next statement, but it's quite true. After flopping with *Bring On the Girls*, I had to move to Hollywood out of fear for my life. What gave this such a bizarre twist is that I was nearly done in as a result of an act of politeness.

To pick up on this painful little episode, we have to go back to the summer of 1924 when I was publicity director for the Paramount Theatres in New York. My boss at the time was an avid fisherman, and to make a long story short, I accepted, against my better judgment and a strong case of dismay, an invitation from him and his wife to spend my vacation fishing at their summer house in Maine.

I don't like fish. I don't like anything about fish, and I certainly wasn't looking forward to getting up at five in the morning to go and catch them. But my hosts were such warm, affectionate, and persistent people, that I just couldn't bring myself to refuse their offer.

I was miserable—as only I can be outside of a metropolitan area—for the entire two weeks. Due to the strain of hay fever that I contracted on that trip, I have been intermittently miserable ever since. The sneezing started on my second day in Maine. Before that I had never been sick a day in my life, even during the 1918 influenza epidemic when the death rate in New York resembled London's during the plague. But apparently something that grows in Maine activated some dormant bugaboo in my system, and thereafter, from May to September, the entire Eastern seaboard declared war on me.

Year by year my situation kept growing worse. Even my mother's chicken soup, surely the most potent concoction since Macbeth's witches stirred their cauldron, proved useless. I'll skip over the unpleasant details except to say that the apex of it came during the summer of 1934 when I sneezed myself into hernia. Shortly before that I had made a quick trip out to Hollywood to cauterize some loose ends to an MGM comedy. While I was there, the sneezing stopped. When I returned, it started. My doctor, one of the most eminent and expensive practitioners in New York, took notice of this, consulted with several other eminent and expensive physicians, and issued his eminent and expensive findings: If I didn't sneeze in California, then why didn't I move out there? And that is how my theatrical career came to a sneezing halt.

Relocating a family from New York to California is no easy task, and I was very grateful that we had so many friends on the receiving end to help us adjust to Hollywood's so very singular *modus vivendi*. Actually, the siren call of the studios had been so tempting that we were just about the last holdouts from our old circle of theatrical friends to make the move.

About a year after I had taken the plunge, the Gershwins folded their tents and joined the caravan. George took a house right next to the one that Ira and Lennore bought on Roxbury Drive, and for an all too brief while, it seemed like old times, perhaps even better. Ira truly loved the easy-going life in the sun, and George seemed to love it even more.

Having spent two years working on something as monumental as *Porgy 'n Bess*, only to see it close after one hundred performances, would have crushed most people, but George, with the help of a succession of the most lovely ladies Hollywood had to offer, appeared to overcome his disappointment with a minimum of anguish. And professionally, George and Ira were to accomplish some of their finest work during those final months out here.

Just as they had been in New York, the parties of the Gershwins were the best in town. At one of these gatherings you would usually find George at the piano, encircled five or six deep. He could play for hours without tiring, and such was his love of performing that it seemed to me the longer he played, the fresher he became.

That was the George that I had always known, brash, dynamic and indomitable, which is what made the final party at Ira's so hauntingly memorable. Over the last few weeks, George had complained of sleeplessness, irritability, loss of coordination, and, above all, headaches. He had seen a number of doctors including a psychiatrist, all of whom could find nothing wrong with him. The consensus that came from this was that George was giving in to that curious form of narcissism/hypochondria that is often found in the movie colony. George came in for a lot of kidding about this, a good deal of it, I'm sorry to say, from me.

George played a few songs at the beginning of the party but soon begged off due to his headache, and for the rest of that evening he sat beside me on a couch. Between complaints about his headache he talked mostly about how he wanted to get back on Broadway. I can't say that I listened with a great deal of sympathy. We all have our troubles, and I was involved with the pressures of writing what turned out to be my most difficult screen assignment and having most of my other time taken up with trying to help get the newly formed Screen Writers Guild on its feet. I had been looking forward to Ira's party as a respite from all of that, but because of George's whining and absence from the piano, the evening was shot.

In a lifetime cobblestoned with self reproachments, the stupidity of the selfish resentment that I felt that night remains supreme.

The next day, a Friday, George took a nap to get some relief from his persistent headache. He lapsed into a coma and never woke up. Exploratory surgery revealed a brain tumor, and George died early that Sunday morning. He was thirty-eight years old.

When I called Ira that day, I was hoping to hear that George was improving. The news that he had passed on hit me like a pole-ax, and even with the passing of all these years, I'm not sure that I'm any better equipped to deal with it now than I was then. The one comfort that I can take is remembering what a zest for living he had. That brassy, "wake up world" dynamism is in all of his music, and we can all take comfort in knowing that George's melodies will be around as long as the forces that run this universe will continue to have men and women falling in love with each other.

George's desire to go back on Broadway was a hope that was shared by almost all of us who had left it for Hollywood. Ira made it back in 1941 with *Lady in the Dark*, which he wrote with Kurt Weill and Moss Hart. My long-delayed return happened a year earlier when I got together with Buddy De Sylva (one of George Gershwin's early lyricists) and Irving Berlin for *Louisiana Purchase*.

Writing *Louisiana Purchase* turned out to be a unique experience in that with most of my projects, I would beat my brains out to come up with a plot and the necessary characters. To come up with this hot potato blintz, all I had to do was to go to breakfast at the old Roosevelt Hotel in New Orleans. I had taken a camera crew down there to shoot some footage of Mardi Gras which would later be used as background for a picture that I was producing. Being from Hollywood carries a certain notoriety, and this led to an introduction to Seymour Weiss, the Roosevelt's manager and inheritor of Huey Long's political machine. While we were having breakfast in the hotel's coffee shop one morning, I asked him if he could recommend a local stockbroker. When I was going through the morning papers, I had noticed that a stock which had nose-dived right after I bought into it had almost made its way back up to the price that I had paid for it. This represented a major windfall for me, and I was anxious to unload it as quickly as possible.

Weiss, who was the epitome of Southern courtliness, said that it would be no problem and invited me up to his office. His secretary placed a call to the broker, but the call that came in was from a senior aide at the White House. This was the time when FDR was meeting some stiff congressional opposition over his attempt to pack the Supreme Court. The Louisiana delegation could have swung it around for the New Dealers, and Weiss was being promised if that did happen, the federal tap would flow freely in patronage-thirsty Louisiana.

Weiss was ecstatic as he hung up the phone. The call from the broker came in, but this was brushed aside as Weiss picked up the phone on his desk that had a direct connection to Governor Leche in Baton Rouge. Within a few seconds, he had the governor on the line, and I heard the whole scheme explained in detail once again. Eventually, my call was put through to the broker, and I left, somewhat shaken by the manipulation of government power that I had just witnessed.

For those of you who might be fuzzy or altogether unfamiliar with this unsavory little episode from our not so distant past, you may rest assured that our system of justice did prevail: FDR didn't get his packed court, and both Seymour Weiss and Governor Leche ended up in prison for misappropriating government funds that were supposed to shore up the economy of their state.

I had to wait almost two years before all of the trials and appeals were completed and all of the details became part of the public record. Even then it was a fine line that I had to walk in order to keep the story from crossing the boundaries of libel, but with a bit of luck and twelve complete rewrites I was able to bring it off. But even if it would have taken twenty-four rewrites, I would have stayed with it. It was just too great a story to pass up, and I desperately wanted to get back on Broadway.

A former collaborator and then neighbor of mine, one Mr. Irving Berlin, was also anxious to get back to Broadway. I've given quite a bit of thought as to what I could say in tribute to this man of such timeless music, and the best answer that comes to mind is to remember that Irving is the man that George Gershwin held in awe.

The ironic thing about this man whose influence on every form of popular music is inestimable is that no one can give a worse presentation of an Irving Berlin song than Irving. He had some sort of device on his piano that allowed him to transpose the notes to the one and only key that didn't perplex him. When he was at home, his playing was passable; when he made the mistake of playing on a different keyboard, he could have kept sailors away from a brothel. And as for his singing, I'll only say that compared to Irving's, my bathtub caterwauls come off like Caruso's. There were a great many looks of dismay when Irving came over that afternoon to play the *Louisiana Purchase* score for a small group of us who were involved in the production, but I wasn't worried. Properly handled, Irving's music will always be incomparable. We still speak on the phone once or twice a year, and I'm happy to report that he sounds as hale and hearty as ever.

I was also very happy to have the opportunity of teaming up once again with Bill Gaxton and Vic Moore. They were at the peak of their popularity then, which accounted for no small part of *Louisiana Purchase* being the hit that it was. Such was the show's success that Paramount snapped up the film rights as a vehicle for Bob Hope. I was originally scheduled to write the screen version, but when Hope's schedule was reshuffled while I was in the midst of a prior commitment, Paramount put Joe Fields (Herb's brother) and his partner Jerome Chodorov on it and rushed it into production.

Despite the immemorable teaming of Bob Hope and Victor Moore, whom the Paramount hierarchy had the good sense to bring to Hollywood for a reprisal of his Senator Loganberry role, plus the studio's lavish technicolor production, I was disappointed in the way *Louisiana Purchase* was brought to the screen. Although we had overcome all potential litigious obstacles with stage version, Paramount wasn't about to take any chances. Not only did they diffuse all of the satiric element in favor of easy laughs, they even went so far as to precede the movie with a disclaimer. That was the only time I've ever seen a movie presented in that way, but I won't belabor the point. Paramount paid me very well for the film rights, which entitled them to protect their investment in the best way they saw fit. This was one of the most valuable lessons that George Kaufman taught me: sometimes you just have to let go.

There are other times when a writer has such an emotional attachment to his creation that no amount of money will induce him to part with it. It was for that reason that *Of Thee I Sing*, the most successful stage musical of the thirties, was never made into a movie.

After the play opened, Groucho very much wanted to play Wintergreen. He worked on Sam Harris, and Sam persuaded George and me to see if it could be turned into a Marx Brothers vehicle. We wrote a treatment, which I recently happened to come across. It would have made a pretty good movie, but it wouldn't have been the same show at all. After that, George and I made a pact with the concurrence of the Gershwins: a) George and I would do the screenplay, b) George would direct, and c) it would star Bill Gaxton and Vic Moore.

We had a number of offers from the studios over the years, but none of them would ever meet with all of our conditions. At one point the bidding reached one million dollars. It was an unprecedented amount at the time, and I've often tried to envision the investment return on my share of it spread over the last fifty years. It's an arresting reflection, especially in light of some of the curves that lay ahead of me, but the memories that linger from that year and a half we spent in the Music Box all those years ago are far too magical for me to have any regrets whatsoever.

CHAPTER SIX

When I went to Hollywood, America was in the midst of a severe depression. The haunting legacy of ten million lives obliterated in a senseless war less than a score of years earlier was still very much on everyone's mind, and the chilling prospect of an even bloodier slaughter was inexorably moving toward the realm of reality with each passing day. To their great credit, the handful of moguls who were then in control of Hollywood made a very determined and largely successful effort to prevent their films from surrendering to the hardness of the times. I certainly had my differences with several of those old pirates, but there was never a time when I didn't respect them for imposing upon the film industry a moral restraint that was genuinely felt and quite separate from any of the strictures that were dictated by the largely redundant Hays Office.

Film aficionados often refer to this period when the studio system of film production was at its peak, circa 1945-55, as the "Golden Age of Hollywood." As a former publicity writer with a few exalted metaphors rattling around in my conscience, I usually experience a reflexive cringe whenever I encounter an era that has been epitomized by a descriptive adjective. Let's face it, as "Golden Ages" go, ten years would seem to be a rather short run of it. However—at this point you should gird yourself for

the standard reactionary grouse about the superiority of
the good old days—when I compare the general tone of
the films representing that bygone Hollywood with what
passes for screen entertainment today, I'm afraid I have
no alternative but to throw in my lot with the nostalgia
buffs.

I know—believe me, I know—that the use of sweeping
generalizations like the preceding usually results in a one-
way trip into the marshes of sentimental quicksand. I
know that there are some very talented and dedicated
writers, actors, and directors who are making quality films
today, even though the film industry is controlled by the
corporate representatives of distant and unfeeling con-
glomerates. I also know—and hasten to add—that a great
deal, perhaps a majority of the films that were produced
during the celebrated "Golden Age" period were, at best,
routine and more often than not, offensively banal. But
at this point I am purposefully stepping back into that
quicksand. Good or bad, the films that were made in the
Hollywood that I knew were connected by a common
thread: they had heart, and they had humor, and they
were made to entertain. Sadly, regrettably, negative ad-
jectives *ad infinitum*, modern filmmakers have found it
desirable to exchange this basic premise of the motion
picture medium, good stories, human concerns, recognizable characters, for the freedom to be violent, vulgar,
and pretentious, to name but a few of the allegedly "rel-
evant" factors that have turned so many of today's movies
into the cinematic equivalent of carnival geek shows.

Well, it appears that I'm proselytizing when I'm supposed to be reminiscing, but Hollywood was a very important part of my life, and it pains me greatly to observe
the wretched extremes that it has taken itself to lately in
the name of entertainment. Here's hoping that the pen-
dulum has reached the furthest degree of its outer arc,
and for the life of me, I can't imagine how it could
possibly go any further.

My entrance into the motion picture business actually began in New York, and I'm grateful to Chico Marx for having made it possible. Chico was an avid member of the New York Bridge Club, where he often played with a number of executives from Paramount Pictures. Through that association a deal was struck in 1929 to film *The Cocoanuts* at Paramount's East Coast studios in Astoria, Queens, on Long Island. The boys originally called for $75,000, which Walter Wanger, who made his producing debut with *The Cocoanuts*, immediately countermanded with an offer of $50,000—take it or leave it. As business manager for the team, Chico personally went to see Adolph Zukor, founder and president of Paramount. When Chico left the meeting, operator extraordinaire that he was, a contract had been signed for the boys to receive $100,000.

George Kaufman and I were asked to adapt our script to a screenplay, but as the mere thought of working on the same material twice brought him to the verge of nausea, the responsibility fell on me. Regretfully, Chico was not my business manager.

Adapting *The Cocoanuts* to a screenplay proved to be one of the easiest assignments of my entire career. As none of us, including our two directors—Paramount wasn't taking any chances and assigned Robert Florey and Joe Santell to co-direct the project—had ever worked on a sound picture before, let alone a sound musical, the filming became a long process of trial and error. No one could decide what a musical should look like, so it was decided to simply film the entire show as it had been done on the stage. Because of that decision we ended up with a three-hour movie of which nearly half the footage was deleted from the final version. This left some pretty jarring lapses in the continuity of the storyline, but as I've stated earlier, the Marx Brothers' vehicles weren't noted for their structural complexity.

Aside from the screenplay, my biggest contribution to the film was convincing Walter Wanger—who had constructed a bandstand on the set—that it wasn't necessary to have the musical numbers filmed in front of a live orchestra. Walter was convinced that the audience would be confused if they couldn't see where the music was coming from. I argued that if the audience would accept a lecherous, red-wigged mute carrying a lit blowtorch in the bottomless pockets of his scruffy overcoat, they wouldn't have any trouble accepting music that could come out of thin air on cue. It took quite a bit of arguing on my part before Walter would relent. When the picture was released it became a very big hit, and as I had been hoping (actually praying—because who could be certain about a thing like that?), the audience accepted the musical innovation without the least bit of difficulty.

The following year I accompanied the Marx Brothers (naturally George Kaufman wasn't involved with the project) back to the same studio for the filming of *Animal Crackers*. This was unquestionably the most enjoyable experience of the four films that I made with the team. Along with *A Night at the Opera* and *Room Service*, both of which were encumbered with some unique problems that I'll elaborate on later, *Cocoanuts* was filmed in an atmosphere of stress and tension.

One of the major problems encountered by the Marx Brothers in the transition from the stage to the screen was learning how to convey their outsized talent through the confines of their new medium. Working before a camera requires staying precisely within predesignated boundaries, and they were used to the freedom of moving about the stage as the energy of the moment directed them. This was especially true of Groucho, whose bobbing in and out of the scene made watching the daily rushes seem like home movies of backyard barbecues.

The frustration that resulted from the boys' awkwardness in front of the camera was exacerbated even further by their fatigue. After spending all day on the set filming *The Cocoanuts*, they would take a cab back into the city for the evening performance of *Animal Crackers*. It was a brutal schedule to maintain, and after a few weeks of it, the boys were so worn down that it was not unusual for swatches of dialogue from *The Cocoanuts* to make their way into the evening performance of *Animal Crackers*.

The combination of the boys' clumsiness and exhaustion led to a great deal of lost time, as take after take was botched and had to be reshot. By the middle of the production they had had enough, and were seriously considering abandoning the project. Fortunately, their sense of professionalism (helped along by an almost certain breach of contract suit) prevailed. Once, however, Chico did walk. It happened on a day when we were trying to film the "land auction" scene. Murphy's Law had governed the morning, and by the time the meal break was called, everyone was in low spirits. When the cast reassembled on the set after lunch, Chico was nowhere to be seen. After a search of the entire Paramount lot still left us with a missing Marx, I acted on a hunch and took a cab to Manhattan where I found him at his bridge club. He was playing a six no-trump hand in a high stakes game, and no amount of cajoling or coercion on my part could budge him from that table. Adolph Zukor be damned, he was never setting foot in that studio again. Thankfully—and I believe I can use that word on behalf of all the Marx Brothers' fans—he overbid himself into a sizable debt before the afternoon was over, and the next morning he was back on the set.

As exasperating as the transition from stage to screen was for the Marx Brothers, the technicians who worked on *The Cocoanuts* had it even worse. Most of the problems revolved around the camera, which was a bulky, cumbersome monster that seemed to have a diabolical tendency to blow fuses only in the midst of scenes that were going well. The solution—as best that my non-technical mind could comprehend it—was found in removing the side panels to prevent a heat build-up around the sensors. Unfortunately, this only led to the problem of what to do about the whirring of the camera's motors, which rever-

berated on the soundtrack so loudly that it all but obliterated the actors' dialogue. After a succession of unsuc-
cessful strategies were applied to the problem, the only
solution that could be found was to encase the entire
apparatus in a soundproof booth. Par for *The Cocoanuts*
course, this in turn led to an even bigger problem.

Due to the heat that is generated by the dozens of
high intensity lamps that are needed to present the actors
at their photogenic best, working on a movie set, at least
those days, was not unlike working in an incubator. We
were filming *The Cocoanuts* during the summer of that
year, and as we were still almost a decade away from air
conditioning, dizzy spells and fainting were a daily occur-
rence on the set. You might well imagine the effect that
the heat had on the poor soul who ran the camera.
Entombed in that airless booth where the temperature
reached 100 degrees by 9 A.M., he would tumble out of it
at the end of every scene, drenched in sweat and gasping
for breath.

To our collective thanks, we didn't have to contend
with any of these problems during the production of
Animal Crackers. The filming took place during the cool-
ness of a pleasant spring, there had been a number of
technical advances made since our first outing, the boys
were much more at ease in front of the camera, and as
their stamina wasn't being taxed by performing another
show at night, they were spared the sense of nervous
exhaustion that had understandably doubled the intensity of all the other problems that had plagued the filming
of *The Cocoanuts*.

The only snafu that did take place during the making
of *Animal Crackers* was a pre-production altercation that
I had with our director, Victor Heerman. When the show
closed on Broadway, the Marx Brothers took it on the
road for a limited tour. During the last month of the run,
I traveled with them, first to Buffalo and then to Cleve-
land. By sitting in the back of the audience at each performance with a copy of the script on one knee and a

notebook on the other, I was able to determine which sections of the show would work well and which ones to omit from the shooting script.

The one area of the show that I was adamant about transferring to the movie version were the musical numbers. I felt that they were necessary to bridge the scenes, but Heerman, who had made his mark as a silent film director, felt otherwise. We got into some pretty heated arguments that went back and forth until we were called into a conference room at the studio for a production meeting. When we got there, the Marx Brothers began pushing the tables and chairs against the wall. When I asked them what they were doing, Groucho said, "We're setting up a boxing ring so that you and Heerman can have this out."

This boxing match, I'm relieved to say, did not take place. I was overruled about including the musical numbers, and in retrospect, it was the correct decision. Heerman felt that comedies should be shorter than dramas, and the soundness of that judgment was an invaluable lesson for which I am indebted to him. He did, however, agree to keep the "Hooray for Captain Spaulding" number, without which I really don't see how we could have done the show. Everyone shook hands, and with the script as a strong basis of support, and being free of the aforementioned problems, we were able to film *Animal Crackers* in the sort of lighthearted atmosphere in which comedy movies should be made, and which, unfortunately, we were never able to duplicate.

It was almost five years before I had a chance to work with the boys again. When *Bring On the Girls* closed during its out-of-town tryouts, Kaufman and I returned to New York to lick our wounds. We spent nearly two months trying to formulate the storyline for another show, but since all of our collaborations aside from our Marx Brothers projects had been political satires, and with that well having suddenly gone dry, nothing usable was ever to materialize.

It was during this non-productive period that Irving
Thalberg, via Zeppo, issued the first of his several invita-
tions to George and me to come to Hollywood and write
A Night at the Opera. Thalberg's offer was an extremely
attractive one, and as our five months investment in *Bring
On the Girls* hadn't returned a dime to us—and as we
seemed to be getting nowhere with a new play—I thought
that we should accept. George had a passionate dislike
for the manner in which the film industry treated its
writers and immediately vetoed the offer.

Over the next two weeks, Zeppo called with two more
offers from Thalberg, each (bless George's intransigence)
more generous than the last, both of which were turned
down by George. At that point Zeppo wired me saying
that in light of George's decision to stay in New York,
Thalberg wanted me to come to Hollywood by myself,
either on a one-picture deal or on a long-term basis.

I very much wanted to continue working with George,
but familial obligation dictated otherwise. My son had
been born that year, and a man with a growing family in
the middle of a severe economic depression just doesn't
turn down a guaranteed income.

When I presented this latest negotiation to George
and asked him to reconsider, he recounted all of the
indignities that he had suffered while writing *Roman Scan-
dals* for Sam Goldwyn, whom he ended up suing over a
salary dispute. The experience had left George so embittered that he had promised never to work in films again.
When I asked him to whom he had solemnly made the
promise, he said, "Myself." This, I assured him, was a
promise which he could probably break without too much
difficulty. He said that he would consider it. That night
he had a long talk with Beatrice, who was finally able to
convince him that there were worse things which could
happen to a person than spending a winter in the California sunshine working on the most lucrative contract that
any screenwriter had yet to receive.

The next morning George called me and spat out an

astringency which he was to repeat to everyone in New York that he subsequently encountered: "All right, damnit, I'll go to Hollywood, but only for a few weeks."

With our original intention being to stay in Hollywood only long enough to write the picture, George and I made the trip without our families. And in hopes of easing the loneliness caused by the separation, we sought the company of our old friends who were staying at the Garden of Allah—the stopping-off place for all of the New York literary expatriates during studio assignments and divorce settlements.

The Garden of Allah was a complex of two-storied, cheaply furnished, two-room bungalows built around a large kidney-shaped swimming pool on the estate of silent film star Alla Nazimova. It is long gone now, replaced—as eventually everything in Los Angeles will be—by a bank. By virtue of his ten-year residence at the Garden of Allah, Robert Benchley became the unofficial host to its cabal of lettered denizens. It was there that Benchley was reputed to have said, following a drunken tumble into the swimming pool: "Get out of these wet clothes and into a dry martini!" The anecdote is apocryphal, but its flavor is certainly reflective of the spirit that prevailed at the Garden of Allah.

The noise, laughter, music, and mating calls were loud and continuous each and every night at the Garden of Allah. It was the reputation of those nocturnal rumblings, by the way, that was responsible for one studio—suspicious that their bleary-eyed employees might be tempted not to turn in a full day's work—having all of the couches removed from the offices of their writers' building. Three sleepless nights in a row were all that Kaufman and I could take, whereupon we packed our bags and moved into the Beverly Wilshire Hotel. We took adjoining suites, and it was there that we wrote *A Night at the Opera*.

The roller coaster pattern of the Marx Brothers' careers found them at their lowest prior to *A Night at the*

Opera. Buoyed by the success that they had achieved with the film version of *Animal Crackers,* they chose to make the rest of their pictures on the Paramount contract—*Monkey Business, Horse Feathers,* and *Duck Soup*—in Hollywood. Herman Mankiewicz was assigned to be their producer, and at his request I did some long distance rewriting on *Monkey Business* and *Horse Feathers.* Today those films are regarded as classics, especially *Duck Soup* which has the Groucho-Harpo mirror sequence, but for some reason they weren't as successful at the box office as the brothers' first two efforts.

Shortly before *Duck Soup* was released, Groucho wrote to me saying that if the movie fared as poorly as the two which preceded it, he was afraid that their contract wouldn't be renewed. It seems very hard to believe that the Marx Brothers' talent could ever have been unwanted, but for nearly a year-and-a-half after *Duck Soup,* no studio would hire them. Their film careers might have ended at that point if Irving Thalberg—another of Chico's bridge partners—hadn't intervened.

Thalberg was a restless, driven man, who thrived on the kind of challenge that the Marx Brothers' reversal proved to be. For that reason, and for that reason alone, they were signed to Hollywood's premier studio over the very highly arched eyebrows of its mogul, Louis B. Mayer.

Before Kaufman and I became involved with *A Night at the Opera,* Thalberg had Bert Kalmar and Harry Ruby, who had previously written *Monkey Business* for the Marxes, and Robert Pirosh and George Seaton who would later give them *A Day at the Races,* each write a script that was structured around a storyline that had been written by James McGuiness, the head of MGM's story department. Both scripts were rejected by Groucho, which was a somewhat brazen act considering the tenuousness of his position. When Thalberg asked him whose script he would accept, Groucho replied, "Kaufman and Ryskind." It was at that point that we began receiving the summons from Zeppo.

When Kaufman and I had written out a storyline that met everyone's approval, George made a quick trip to New York to attend to some business matters. I started working on the script, and when I had finished the first scene where Groucho meets Maggie Dumont in the restaurant, I took it to Thalberg to show him the work in progress. The scene was only a couple of pages long, and when I gave it to him, he read through its entire length without the faintest smile crossing his face. When he was finished he handed it back to me and said, "Morrie, that's the funniest scene that I have ever read." I've always wondered what his reaction would have been if he hadn't liked it.

When George returned from New York, we locked into the writing of the script, which only took us a little over a month to complete. I could attribute the ease with which we sailed through the writing process to our familiarity with the Marxes. I could even cite George's burning desire to be finished with the assignment as an added impetus. Both particulars were of great benefit to us, but—to our simultaneous gratitude and embarrassment— the biggest factor that was working in our favor was that Zeppo was no longer a part of the act. His part was filled by screen newcomer Allan Jones, whose good looks and excellent voice gave his characterization a dimension that allowed us to advance the story in ways that Zeppo would never have been able to fulfill. I was especially fond of Mr. Jones' "Alone" duet with Kitty Carlisle, unquestionably the finest musical number of all the Marx Brothers' projects.

The day after we finished writing the script, George Kaufman remained true to his word by packing his bags and returning to New York. At Thalberg's request, I remained with the production. During one of his innumerable production meetings, Thalberg made mention of his plans to hold a sneak preview of the completed film. Judging a film's strengths and weaknesses prior to its general release by showing it to a paying audience in a small town away from Los Angeles was a Thalberg innovation, which proved to be an important element in his winning track record. While there was certainly no denying the merits of the advance screening process, it seemed to me that it would be of an even greater benefit to the production if we could go through the trial and error procedure before the filming began, as we had done by taking *Animal Crackers* on tour. When I mentioned the possibility of incorporating major scenes from the script into stage show, Thalberg concurred, and shortly afterwards the Marx Brothers, Allan Jones, Maggie Dumont, and myself began a five-stop tour starting in Salt Lake City.

At Thalberg's insistence, we were accompanied on the tour by Al Boasberg, a very successful gag writer who wrote a great deal of Jack Benny's materials. Although we were respectful of each other's work, Mr. Boasberg and I didn't get along very well personally. It's hard to be specific about the reasons, but they were entirely personal and not professional and I would be remiss in not acknowledging a number of very funny contributions—especially the business in the stateroom scene—that he made to the script.

The first week of the tour was a disaster. As the boys had been absent from the stage for over five years, they were understandably nervous. They missed cues and stepped on each other's lines, but the biggest problem during those ill-fated performances in Salt Lake City was the overly aggressive manner in which Groucho presented himself. His confidence had been seriously (and understandably, although far more than I had realized until then) undermined by the loss of the Paramount contract. Unable to relax, he unconsciously began to commit one of the cardinal sins of performing: overcompensation. He was so wound up that whenever he would deliver a line it was almost as if he were saying to the audience, "This material is funny and you'd better laugh." Faced with a militant challenge like that, very few of them did.

We made a number of changes in the script before the show opened in Seattle. The audience began to respond much more favorably to us, and the combination of the two went a long way in helping Groucho regain the confidence that was so essential to the character that he had spent a lifetime developing. After playing Portland and San Francisco, we ended up in Santa Barbara with a script—and a Groucho—that were in much better shape than the ones we opened with in Salt Lake City. The tour worked out very well, and I shudder to think what the consequences would have been if we hadn't made it. When it was over, we felt that we were onto something special and were anxious to get it before the cameras.

Movies are like politics in that they oftentimes make for some very strange bedfellows; none perhaps stranger than the pairing of Sam Wood and the Marx Brothers.

Sam was one of the master directors of that era, with an astonishing list of credits that ranged from several of Gloria Swanson's silent films to *A Night at the Opera* and its successor *A Day at the Races*, to *Our Town*, *Kitty Foyle*, *King's Row*, *The Pride of the Yankees*, *For Whom the Bell Tolls*, *Command Decision*, *Goodbye Mr. Chips*, and a large portion of *Gone With the Wind* which Sam directed without taking credit.

As one might surmise from reading that impressive list of mostly dramatic works (excluding his two Marx Brothers' projects), Sam was a very orderly man who projected a great sense of sober purpose about himself. To the Marx Brothers, who had just come off the tryout tour in exceptionally high spirits, Sam's solemnity was a welcome inspiration for the relentless series of practical jokes that surpassed their long history of assaults on Margaret Dumont. He was pickpocketed, locked out of his car, barricaded from entering the soundstage, and on several occasions found himself the consumer of lunches containing some very suspect ingredients. Since he was already suffering from an aggravated ulcer, Sam was prone to flare up over these pranks, which led to a great deal of friction between the director and his stars. Consequently, I found myself spending more time trying to smooth down ruffled egos than I did tending to the script.

The tension that grew out of that clash of temperaments between Sam and the boys was exasperated even further by the inordinate amount of time it took to complete the filming. Sam shot each scene from virtually every conceivable angle and then ordered multiple takes, in many instances thirty or more, for each set-up. What none of us knew at the time was that the repetitiveness was in accordance with Thalberg's instructions. By having such an excess of footage to choose from in the editing process, Thalberg had assured himself of being able to put his personal stamp on the picture without having to be on the set during production. It was a very expensive and unnecessary manner in which to make a film, and the enmity that resulted from it had a great deal to do with my turning down the offer of a long-term contract at MGM.

Despite all of the problems that occurred during the production, *A Night at the Opera* turned out to be not only MGM's biggest hit of 1935, but, at least in my opinion, the best of the Marx Brothers' screen efforts. Although Groucho was to spend the rest of his days denying it, Sam Wood's contribution to that accomplishment can't be overlooked. Comedy may not have his metier, but what he lacked in comic instinct he more than made up for with his sure-handed craftsmanship, which is exactly what the Marx Brothers needed at that juncture of their careers.

In turn, it can also be said that the Marx Brothers were as good for Sam as he was for them. *A Night at the Opera* was his first smash hit in sound films, and he was able to use it as a springboard for his subsequent successes. There wasn't any love lost between Sam and the Marxes, but I do know that it was to everyone's mutual satisfaction when Sam signed on as both producer and director of their next film, *A Day at the Races*.

Personally, I had a tremendous respect for Sam's ability as a director and an even higher respect for him as a man. He was a lifelong Republican who was—if such a thing is possible—even more conservative then than I am now. (Groucho said of him, "He's so far to the right he's coming around again on the left.") After the war, Sam spearheaded the fight in Hollywood against the Communists, and I've always been rather proud of the fact that my shift to the right-of-center began as a result of my association with him.

I was anxious to return to New York when we finally completed the filming of *A Night at the Opera*, but as it was then late summer, when the pollen count is at its highest there, just looking at a copy of the *New York Times* was enough to send me into a paroxysm of sneezing. Zeppo—Hollywood's most aggressive agent—suggested that I take on a short-term assignment until it was safe to go home. I agreed, and a few days later he had me signing a contract to do a rewrite job on *Ceiling Zero* at Warner Brothers.

Ceiling Zero was an aviation story that had been written by Frank "Spig" Wead. He was an excellent writer—*Test Pilot, Dive Bomber, They Were Expendable*—and a remarkable man whose real life story was as heroic as anything that he created. A career naval officer, he had been an ace test pilot until a spinal injury from a freak accident left him with severely limited use of his legs. Despite this tremendous obstacle (and there were times during our partnership when I wondered where he found the courage to go on), he continued to write articles and stories that were of enormous benefit to the revitalization of the navy's air wing prior to World War II. When the war did break out, Commander Wead, with a brace on each leg and a cane in each hand, sailed into combat aboard one of the escort carriers that he had been largely responsible for getting Congress to build for the navy. What I thought to be one of the best of the John Ford/John Wayne movies, *On the Wings of Eagles*, was based on Commander Wead's life.

The storyline of *Ceiling Zero* was centered around an abrasive airmail pilot who redeems himself for having caused the death of a fellow pilot by sacrificing himself on a fatal mission testing wing de-icers. It was a very well written story, and had the picture been made by any director other than Howard Hawks, it could have been filmed exactly as Wead had written.

The average rate of speaking is around 150 words per minute. This roughly translates to one page of dialogue equaling one minute of performance on the screen. In the typical Hawksian movie, however, that ratio had to be doubled. This was especially the case with *Ceiling Zero*, which starred James Cagney and Pat O'Brien, both of whom could rattle off dialogue with the casual aplomb of tobacco auctioneers.

My job, as I quickly realized to my amused consternation, was to somehow stretch the story to nearly double its original length, without becoming redundant in the process. It wasn't easy. Howard Hawks attended all of our writing sessions, and as he had been a pilot in World War I, there were times when I couldn't help but feel out of place.

At that point in my life, my aerial experience consisted of a single, near-disastrous open-cockpit flight which I reluctantly undertook at the urging of Groucho, and after which I concluded with a vow that I would never go aloft again. I had no comprehension whatsoever of the aeronautical jargon that Wead and Hawks bandied about; until Wead explained it to me, I didn't even understand the meaning of "ceiling zero" (the altitude of the prevailing cloud cover over an airfield)—which was, to my great embarrassment, a great deal different from "sealing zero"— my first impression when Zeppo mentioned it to me over the telephone.

When my technical ignorance had fully manifested itself, the three of us concluded that they would do all of the necessary rewriting about "slip streams," "negative G forces," and I would concentrate on injecting some hu-

mor into the human element of the story. From that
arrangement came a script that Hawks was able to turn
into a movie that buffs of the aviation genre seem to
regard as something of a milestone. Warner Brothers
also seemed to have a high regard for it. They remade it
twice, once as *International Squadron* with Ronald Reagan.

It was after I had finished working on *Ceiling Zero* that
my wife and I decided to make our home in California.
By the time we returned to New York to settle our affairs,
and then returned to Los Angeles to select and settle into
our new home, nearly five months had been spent in the
accommodation of our decision. When the dust from our
transcontinental dervish had settled down, I was very
anxious to get back to work. My friends from New York
had given me stern warnings about the dangers of working in Hollywood. The consensus was that after spending
a year performing what they laughingly referred to as
"work" in Hollywood, my brain would atrophy to the
consistency of mush. As it turned out, however, the hard-
est phase of my professional life was just beginning.

CHAPTER SEVEN

When I'm asked what Hollywood was like during its heyday, I've always felt it best to fall back on that time-tested commencement speech bromide about the blindfolded natives who touch different parts of an elephant and perceive it in different ways. For some—almost all New Yorkers—Hollywood was nothing more than a bejeweled chamber pot attended by overpaid morons. For others, Hollywood indeed was the pot at the end of the rainbow. My own perception falls somewhere between those two factions and is probably best illustrated by the circumstances surrounding the making of a little schnitzel I refer to as "my Lubitsch picture."

Almost every writer that I knew wanted Ernst Lubitsch, of the justly famed "Lubitsch touch," to direct his pictures. My opportunity came during the war when I frequently found myself working for 20th Century-Fox. My first assignment there was *Claudia*, which was based on Rose Franken's hit play. It was such a well-crafted work that all I had to do was put it in cinematic terms and stay out of its way. In fact, it turned out to be such an easy project to complete that I almost (the accent being on the adverb) felt guilty about accepting my salary.

Normally it would take me about twelve weeks to knock out a screenplay, but because of the ease with which *Claudia* lent itself to cinematic terms, I was able to finish it in about half that time. Because I had some extra time on my hands, Bill Perleberg, who had produced *Claudia*, asked me to have a go at *The Meanest Man in the World*. This was a Jack Benny picture based on a play by George M. Cohan. They had already filmed it, but no one was pleased with the results. The last half of the story seemed the weakest part to me, and after I rewrote it, Lubitsch, who was then recuperating from one of the several heart attacks that finally did him in, agreed to direct it as a way of easing back into his work schedule.

Ernst and I hit off terrifically, and by the time our retooling chores on *The Meanest Man in the World* were finished, we had made a pact to work together on a full collaboration one day. With that thought playing merry with my Muse, I sat down and penned *Where Do We Go from Here?* And while Zeppo took the script and began squeezing some hemoglobin out of the executive turnips at Fox, I sent a copy over to Lubitsch who called back with a word that he would love to direct it.

Having a commitment from Ernst Lubitsch put me in one of the most enviable positions in Hollywood, but my good fortune was quickly shot down by Bill Perleberg. He had been assigned to produce the picture, and he argued that he had spent twenty years building up his reputation in the film industry, but if Ernst Lubitsch were the director, it would automatically become an Ernst Lubitsch picture. So with Ernst out, the directing assignment went to the Russian raconteur, director, and sometime character actor Gregory Ratoff simply because he had lost $50,000 to Darryl Zanuck in a poker game, and the only way Zanuck could get it was to put Ratoff on the payroll and garnish his wages. Overall, I have to say that Ratoff did a pretty good job out of it, but it was not the movie that I had originally envisioned.

Every screenwriter that I knew could have offered up a similar experience about not having their immortal words treated with the reverence that they deserved. Frustrating though it sometimes could be, the one thing that none of us who were working in Hollywood at that time could deny was just that—work was available to anyone who could push a noun against a verb in a sequence that an actor could repeat to an engaging effect.

After making *A Night at the Opera*, I was offered a seven-year contract at MGM. To have signed and seen that contract through its completion would have meant financial security for my family for the rest of our days. Tempting though it was, I preferred to take my chances as a free-lancer. This gave me not only the freedom to pick and choose those projects with which I felt compatible, but more importantly it meant that I could work on them at home where I wouldn't be thought eccentric by anyone except my wife, who had long since resigned herself to having an unshaven man in his pajamas and bathrobe muttering incoherently as he paced back and forth all day, and oftentimes all night long.

Although I did pay a price for my freedom, Hollywood was still a very lucrative game to play. During the twelve years that I was active in the movies, I wrote about fifteen scripts and rewrote about twice that number. A lot of established writers felt that script doctoring was beneath them, but as one who could never fix anything with his hands, I would always draw a great deal of pleasure from being able to step in and help shore up a weak scenario. This could vary all the way from being asked to polish up just one particular scene, to performing a complete evisceration and starting again from scratch. And here again I feel it necessary to reiterate my contention that having had the freedom of artistic choice led to better writing, which in turn led to better movies, although *Rhythm on the Range* put a hell of a curve in that equation.

Should you have been lucky enough to never have *Rhythm on the Range* pop up on your late night TV screen, this was an opus which had Bing Crosby traveling across the country in a box car with a prized bull that he was frequently compelled to serenade.

I did a lot of rewriting for Crosby (with a lot better results, I'm happy to inform), a couple of those projects being when he was teamed up with Bob Hope and Dorothy Lamour for the "Road" pictures. This was during the period when America was involved in all that unpleasantness with the Huns. Simplifying the plot to as few settings as possible was the standing order at that time due to an edict by the War Production Board which drastically reduced the amount of material that could be used for set constructions. And while the "Road" pictures might not have been given the best of production values, they were a blast to do. The Hope/Crosby act was as funny off camera as it was on, and I'll wager that many a nightclub owner would have been happy to have had half the number of paying customers in their establishments as there were visitors crowded onto those Paramount sound stages when Messrs. H and C were going at each other.

The most memorable rewriting assignment that I ever took on was at the invitation of Howard Hawks when he remade *The Front Page* as *His Girl Friday*. As a rule I've never had much of a regard for movie remakes, but this speeding bullet romp through the woollier side of Chicago's fourth estate certainly proved to be a cracker jack exception. I thought it was not only the best of *The Front Page's* three screen incarnations, but it was also the best film I've ever seen about the newspaper racket. I should also like to add that *His Girl Friday* remains in my opinion as the best film of Howard Hawks' career—at least of the ones where the sound of gunfire didn't surpass the Battle of the Marne. Howard loved stories that were compressed into a brief time span and could be told quickly, and with this one, he set what must surely be the movies' all time pacing record.

Aside from the verbal blitzkrieg that the cast perpetrated, what gave *His Girl Friday* its distinction was Howard's inspired notion of transmogrifying the Hildy Johnson character into Hilda, the ace reporter and former wife of the despotic editor Walter Burns, played so expertly by Rosalind Russell and Cary Grant. This is where it got tricky. The ending of the script that I was given had remained (with only a slight bow to the gender change) faithful to the original Hecht/MacArthur premise of Walter Burns giving Hildy a goodbye present of his watch and then phoning the police to have him taken off the train with—"That son of a b— stole my watch." Howard felt that with the success of *The Front Page's* run on Broadway and the equally successful first screen version that the ending had lost its punch. I opted for a new set of circumstances and tag line with which Howard was very pleased. As it turned out, so was someone else.

His Girl Friday was made for Columbia Pictures. One evening after work I happened to stop in a small establishment near the studio that Columbia's contract writers used as a winding down station before venturing back out into reality. When the conversation came around to me I mentioned the new ending that I had come up with. A few days later, I was crossing the studio lot when a writer who was in the bar that night stopped to inform me that he had just come from a sound stage where he observed my ending being filmed as the closing on another film. Apparently another writer in the bar that night had some very opaque notions about what constituted public domain. At first I didn't believe it, but a trip to the projection room to view the day's rushes put quite a crimp in that thought. There on the screen, with just enough changes to make it legal, was the scene that was supposed to wrap up *His Girl Friday*.

When I finished with my fulminations, and quite extensive they were at that, my only option was to write yet another ending. With the original or any variation of it no longer feasible, I devised the one of a guarded marital reconciliation between Walter and Hildy. This was kept under wraps until Howard filmed it. Both Howard and I agreed that the romantic flavor of the new ending worked out better than our previous one, so in a way, I'm grateful

to that writer at Columbia—who shall remain anonymous—
for giving us the impetus to make a great film even
better. My only regret now is that the fellow "what done
me wrong" at Columbia wasn't around on a couple of
other pictures when I could have used him.

As interesting and rewarding as the rewriting assignments were, a career is based on acknowledged credits,
and of all the films that bore my name, the greatest
satisfaction came from the two that I made with Gregory
La Cava: *My Man Godfrey* and *Stage Door.*

A few years ago, I happened to receive an inquiry
from an overly earnest (is there any other kind?) young
film scholar asking me to assist him with some insight
into the allegorical implications of *My Man Godfrey.* As
best that I could understand his request, the young man
was constructing his thesis around the fact that the title
character of Godfrey Parke, the millionaire turned depression bum who takes a job as a butler to a wealthy
family on Fifth Avenue and then uses his acumen to save
the family from financial ruin, was supposed to be a
representation of God. The key to understanding this
assertion could be found in Godfrey's name. Godfrey
had brought love to the wealthy family, hence the name
GOD-Free, and wasn't it artistic of me to have devised such
a meaningful idea? Well, as all of this came as news to me,
the most that I could do for the young man was write
back to him and inquire if he were certain that we were
discussing the same movie.

The desire to read some sort of symbolic message
into the films of the thirties, when our only intent was to
entertain, strikes me as a very strange endeavor. Over the
years I've received a number of similar requests, most of
which revolve around whether or not the Marx brothers
were meant to be representatives of the world's nameless
masses striking a blow of freedom against the unfeeling
upper crust of society. To this, I always respond with a
smile and an unequivocal "no." The Marx Brothers were
simply vaudeville performers who switched from singing

to comedy when they realized that a laughing audience could be a great deal more beneficial to them than a booing audience when it came time to square up with their creditors. The act worked, and they very wisely stayed with it for the rest of their careers.

As for *My Man Godfrey*, this wistful little tale from Eric Hatch's novel, *1011 Fifth Avenue*, was based partly on fact. There were numerous incidents of the Wall Street crash of '29 turning millionaires into clerks, laborers, and even butlers, when they could find a position. (What was left of New York's monied set seemed to prefer the cachet that came from having former Russian aristocrats who had fled the Bolshevik revolution butle for them.) As for the movie's title, it was originally to have been the same as the novel. The change was made from *1011 Fifth Avenue* to *My Man Godfrey* in deference to the leading man requisites of Mr. William Powell, whose services we had the very unexpected pleasure of obtaining.

Universal Pictures had obtained the screen rights to *1011 Fifth Avenue* with the express hope of signing Constance Bennett to play the role of the addle-brained heiress Irene Bullock. Universal was then teetering on the edge of bankruptcy and in dire need of the kind of box office hit that Constance Bennett's presence would insure. Miss Bennett was indeed one of the industry's biggest money makers at the time, and no one was more aware of the fact or of the prerogatives that come with it than she, as Greg La Cava was soon to discover.

Because of his bifurcated reputation of being a brilliant director and a constant torment to whoever was brave enough to hire him, Greg La Cava bounced back and forth between Hollywood's studios like a pinball. One of his assignments landed him at 20th Century-Fox where he was able to channel Constance Bennett's tempestuous energies into a superior performance in *The Affairs of Cellini*. On the basis of that accomplishment, and I'm afraid for that reason alone, Greg was asked to direct *1011 Fifth Avenue*.

Greg was anxious to accept the Universal's offer, but the battle scars from *The Affairs of Cellini* had left him little desire for an encore encounter with Miss Bennett. In her stead, Greg hoped to use Claudette Colbert, whom he had just had such a great success directing in *She Married Her Boss* for Columbia (whose gates closed behind him with a pronounced finality). To secure Miss Colbert's participation, Greg utilized the Machiavellian-like ploy of agreeing to direct Miss Bennett, but only on the condition that William Powell be brought in as the co-star. The reasoning behind this was that by making a demand which he knew would be an impossibility to meet, Universal would then owe him a concession—exit Miss Bennett, enter Miss Colbert.

At that time it did seem impossible that William Powell, whose stature at MGM was second only to Clark Gable's, would agree to loan out at Universal, which had supplanted Columbia at the southern end of the pecking order of the major studios, whose financial collapse was being forecast on a daily basis. But to everyone's amazement, and no one more so than La Cava, Powell agreed to play Godfrey, conditional on Carole Lombard being brought in from Paramount to be "his" co-star. The executives at Universal had no difficulty in recognizing the advantages of acquiring a star of Miss Bennett's magnitude without acquiring Miss Bennett's penchant for provoking tensions and were only too happy to accommodate Mr. Powell's proviso. It naturally followed that as William Powell was deemed a bigger star than Carole Lombard, then the emphasis of the story—which had the part of the butler being secondary to that of the heiress—would now have to be reversed. This is what led to our new title, and if anyone can draw any allegorical implications from that, I urge them not to miss Harpo's representation of the Anti-christ in *Animal Crackers*.

Off-camera, William Powell and Carole Lombard were exactly as they appeared on screen, which made working with them the sort of hoot that makes usage of "working"

seem a falsehood. He with his flair for wry understatement and she with her blonde brassiness went at each
other for the course of the entire production, but it was
obvious for all to see that their insults were only a cover-
up for a deeply felt affection. I suppose that along with
everyone else, I often found myself wondering how it was
they could go through a divorce and remain such good
friends. The most that Carole would ever volunteer about
the subject was a shrug and "It's better this way." William
Powell was even more reserved about the matter, but
once he did tell me that his sole purpose for taking the
part was to insure that Carole obtained the role that he
felt (correctly) would solidly establish her as a major star.

While there is no disputing the enormous box office
appeal that was generated by the combined Powell/
Lombard stardom, I do not wish to overlook the contributions of the Pirandellian perfection of our supporting
cast, I still feel it necessary to attribute the ultimate success of *My Man Godfrey* to Greg La Cava. That being
stated, I also feel it necessary to make a qualification. I
dislike delving into the private lives of those who are no
longer here to speak for themselves, but it would be
impossible to discuss Greg's work without mentioning
the effect, both good and bad, that was the result of his
drinking problem. He was an alcoholic. Having made this
moral trespass, I can at least take some comfort in the
fact that it reads somewhat softer than Pandro Berman's
(RKO's production chief) appraisal, "He's a drunken
bum," which was pretty much the sentiment of every
studio head that Greg worked for. Be that as it may,
Gregory La Cava, with his remarkable sense of comic
timing and his refined flair for improvisation, still remains in my opinion as the finest comedy director that I
ever worked with.

As a partnership, Greg and I hit off from the word go.
There were a number of reasons for this, the most welcome among them being that the disdain that Greg held
for most conventions also extended to his regard for the

standard screenplay format. If you've ever seen a screenplay from that era, with their stultifying preponderance
of scene numbers, CAPITAL LETTERS, and camera directions, you would have no trouble in understanding
why this was such a blessing:

> 237 INT. OPERA HOUSE–NIGHT–ESTABLISHING
> SHOT From
>
> Groucho's P.o.V., CAMERA trucks into med. two
> shot of Harpo and
>
> Chico–followed by 180 degree CAMERA LEFT PAN
> to pick up entrance of Mrs. Claypool.

Even though this tended to make scripts read like
engineering manuals, the prevailing wisdom of the industry had declared the form inviolable and this is what
proved to be the undoing of so many writers. If I thought
of it in terms of mechanics, I too was stopped, but by
approaching it from the perspective of a student applying
an algebraic theorem, I could manage to get by. When we
worked on *A Night at the Opera*, I tried to help George
Kaufman with this method, but he refused to even consider dealing with "that dam camera gibberish." One of
the few conversations that I had with F. Scott Fitzgerald
was taken up with this same subject. In Fitzgerald's case,
it was doubly sad, as he had made a very determined
effort to come to grips with this alien craft, but after four
years of trying he was to have but a single screen credit.

As Greg didn't require camera directions to be written down, "I wouldn't use them anyway," all I had to do
was tell the story as simply and clearly as I could. Had I
not been able to take this shortcut, I seriously doubt that
Godfrey would have been made.

There has long been an argument in Hollywood over
the consequences of allowing novelists and playwrights to
adapt their own works to the screen. I'm afraid that Mr.
Hatch, who had made the movie rights to his story pro-
visional on his being allowed to write the first draft of the
screenplay, set a bad example for anyone who might wish

to take up the cause on behalf of all the authors who have decried the fate of their creations in the hands of us "Hollywood hacks." Mr. Hatch did write a very good novel, whatever happened to him afterward I couldn't say, but when I was shown his completed draft, it became very obvious very quickly that his instincts were literary not cinematic. With the exception of the page numbers, nothing from the original had been omitted. All of the prose had been converted into dialogue, which, coupled with dialogue that already existed, resulted in a script that, had it been filmed as written, would have played like one of those marathons that Eric Von Stroheim used to make.

Considering that it was less than a month before the production was supposed to begin, Greg didn't seem terribly bothered about this. After handing me a copy of the original book, he merely smiled and said, "We're all expecting something very nice from you." I appreciated this confidence, but I can't say I was overly pleased about the time squeeze that I had to contend with in order to justify it. When the actual filming began I only had the first half done, and for the next few weeks after that, it took every ounce of concentration that I could muster to stay ahead of the production as it kept closing in on me.

About midway into the filming I did get caught up short, but it was from circumstances over which I had no control.

Greg was a member of a notorious drinking cabal that included John Barrymore and W. C. Fields, both of whom arrived on the set one Saturday afternoon to wait for Greg. Barrymore seemed much more subdued than his reputation would suggest but Fields was a ripsnorting replica of his screen persona. When we were introduced, he greeted me with, "Ah, yes, the little Hebrew scribe," and then proceeded to make an examination of his fingers to make sure that he hadn't lost any in the handshakes. When we knocked off that afternoon, the three of them set off on a bender which landed Greg in the hospital the next day.

On Monday morning, our executive producer Charles Rogers was bursting with livid retrospections about having hired Greg. After announcing that he had been fired, he asked (ordered) me to take over as director. The production was on a very tight schedule due to William Powell's commitment to begin filming a sequel to *The Thin Man* just three weeks after the projected date of *Godfrey*'s wrap-up. There couldn't be any delay, and as I was the one closest to the story, the production was now in my hands. Whether I was closest to the story or not, the transition from the writer's cubicle to the director's chair was one that I wasn't prepared to make. I might have been able to direct a stage play where I would only have to contend with actors, but all of this business with the lights and camera lens was completely beyond the province of my ability.

In an effort to forestall what surely would have been a fiasco, I suggested (pleaded) that we wait at least a week before taking any action. Greg had always been able to rebound from his spells before, and I still had several days work yet to do on the script. Although William Powell could see the wisdom of my not attempting a directorial debut with an unfinished script, the delay would eat into his vacation time, and that prospect moved him to a fit of grousing that was very uncharacteristic of him. After an impassioned entreaty by Charles Rogers, he reluctantly agreed, but I believe that if the truth were known, for Carole Lombard's sake he would have worked right up until the day he was to report back to MGM.

Rogers made an announcement to the press that the production would be shut down for a week while Greg recuperated from the flu. I seriously doubt that this fooled anyone, but it did give me the opportunity to engage myself in a few all-night sessions which saw the script through to its completion. On Friday of that week, the fervent praying that I had suddenly become reacquainted with was answered; Greg would be discharged from the hospital the following day and would return to work on

Monday. On Sunday, Greg came to my house for a "script consultation." This was nothing more than a meaningless gesture to appease the Universal hierarchy, but as long as it contributed to my being taken off the hook, I was more than willing to go through the motions.

Outwardly, Greg didn't appear to be any worse for the wear, but as we talked, a noticeable edginess began to overtake him. About fifteen minutes into our talk, he suddenly slammed his hand on the table, "What's a man have to do to get offered a drink in this place?" I supposed that I could have rooted around in one of the pantry shelves and come up with a bottle of something, but it hardly seemed like a sound idea to be offering a drink to a man who had just spent a week shaking off the heebie jeebies. When I apologized with, "Sorry, Greg, there's not a drop in the house," he exploded. "What are you, a Jewish Mormon?" I tried to smile this off and bring his thoughts back to the script, but he wouldn't be placated. "I passed a couple of stores coming over here," he said with a glint of Dickensian glee lighting up his face, "we can send out for something." I reminded him about the Sunday liquor laws, but the concept was apparently too foreign for him to grasp. At that point there didn't seem to be anything left to be gained by tactfulness, so I just told him straight out that with all the jobs that were at stake, I wasn't about to be party to his going back in the padded room with the imaginary spiders crawling on the walls. I was just starting to get wound up in my spiel when he cut my pontifications short with, "All right. All right, give me a damn coke," which I did, and which he accepted with the distaste of a man being offered radioactive waste.

I wish that I could report that my little lecture had some sort of positive effect on Greg's problem, but the next morning on the set, the coffee cup (a ruse that he was employing long before anyone had ever heard of Jackie Gleason) was on the stand beside his chair. Thankfully, his drinking pals maintained a judicious distance and Greg was able to keep himself in balance until he finished directing the film that would become the biggest box office hit that Universal had scored until that time.

A runaway hit of *My Man Godrey*'s nature has a way of invoking a lot of forgiveness. Universal responded in kind by making Greg some very generous offers. Greg responded in character by going on a celebratory binge that landed him back in the padded room, and Universal quietly decided that they could get along without Mr. La Cava.

After re-emerging from his post-*Godfrey* situation, Greg signed on with RKO, and after a few of my own misadventures at Universal (more than this anon), I caught up with him about six months later.

RKO was the smallest of the seven major studios, which helped—especially during Pan Berman's stewardship—to give it a family-like atmosphere. For that reason I was always happy—at least until Pan Berman left—to land an assignment there. Although the studio itself consisted of only a few sound stages on a lot adjacent to the sprawling Paramount complex, its output in terms of quality more than made up for its lack of quantity: *Little Women, Morning Glory, King Kong, Bringing Up Baby, Bachelor Mother, Gunga Din, Kitty Foyle, Citizen Kane, The Magnificent Ambersons*, and *Suspicion*, to name a few. But with all due respect to the impressive roster of classics, I felt that RKO's greatest distinction came from its impressive series of musicals with Fred Astaire and the ever so delectable Ginger Rogers.

I really wanted to work on one of the A/R's (and who wouldn't?), which sort of became a reality as my first project at RKO. They gave me a story with a New York setting to adapt, but my involvement ended after only two very enjoyable weeks of working on the script. Just when I got to the scene where I had Fred and Ginger dancing on top of the Empire State Building, La Cava learned that we were both working for the same studio. He asked Pandro Berman to have me reassigned to his project, and before I knew what hit me, I was back in the midst of another La Cava mixmaster.

Despite all the pressures that were automatically associated with Greg's scattershot approach to film making—and this one got so topsy turvy that *Life* magazine came in to do a spread on us—I was glad, in the end, to have been a part of *Stage Door*, in that it gave me a chance to say everything I had ever wanted to say about Broadway: the good, the bad, the ugly, and the beautiful. It also gave me a chance to work with Andrea Leeds, Ann Miller, Gail Patrick, Constance Collier, Eve Arden, and Lucille Ball in support of Ginger Rogers and Katharine Hepburn, and if there has ever been a greater cast of female talent assembled for one movie, I've yet to see it.

Ostensibly, *Stage Door* was to be based on the play that George Kaufman rushed back to New York to write with Edna Ferber when our collaboration on *A Night at the Opera* was finished. Tony Veiller, one of the best writers in the business, had made an adaptation, but Greg was unhappy over it being too faithful to the original. I hadn't seen the play, but when I read the script I could understand why.

The plot of *Stage Door* was taken up with struggles of two would-be Broadway actresses sharing a room at a third-rate boarding house. One of them perseveres against all odds and becomes a star, while the other was shown to be selling out her virtue by going to Hollywood. This was one of George's favorite themes, and as he had already worked it over pretty well with Marc Connelly in *Merton of the Movies* and with Moss Hart in *Once in a Lifetime*, I felt that it had lost most of its bite. I loved Broadway, but my experiences there hadn't convinced me that Hollywood had a monopoly on compromises, con artists, and prima donnas. Greg asked me if I could rewrite the opening scene from that perspective. Since the production was scheduled to begin in less than a week, I figured that this was all that would be asked of me and then I could get back to the Astaire/Rogers project.

What I did like about *Stage Door* was the girls' theatrical hotel where most of the story takes place. The Footlights Club, as Kaufman and Ferber had it, was loosely based on the Rehearsal Club which was still in existence on West 58th Street until just a few years ago. During my bachelor days, I had begun many a date in the Rehearsal Club's lobby, and from the memory of the girls' wisecracks to each other as they went up and down the main staircase came the scene that I presented to La Cava a few days later. He looked the pages over for a few minutes and then said, "This is great! Now go home and get started on the rest of it, because I'm going to shoot this on Thursday."

It was to go that way for the entire production, and when we were finished, the only thing that remained from the original Kaufman/Ferber story was the title. In order to come up with a new plot and dialogue, I had to work on the script all day at the studio and most of the night at home. And even with that effort, I was never to be more than a one day ahead of the filming, and there were many times when everybody had to stand around and wait while I sat off to one side of the set feverishly trying to finish the next scene.

None of the cast had ever worked that way before, and it seemed to be especially hard on Katharine Hepburn, who was used to long rehearsal periods. About midway into the shoot she stopped me and asked, "Morrie, how is this going to end? Do I get Dolf or does Ginger?" It was a valid question, but the best answer I could give her at the time was, "Don't ask me that now, Kate, because I'm just not that far ahead yet."

There were similar apprehensions emanating from the head office, but when the rushes were screened each day, everyone agreed that although we didn't know exactly where we were going with this story, we were definitely headed in the right direction.

By the way, the Dolf that Miss Hepburn made reference to was, of course, that inimitable cad of all cads,

Adolph Menjou, who held up the male end of *Stage Door* by himself. We became close friends during the filming, and like everyone else that came within the periphery of that modern Beau Brummel's sartorial splendor, to know him was to suffer in comparison. Whenever he could visit our house, my wife would make a great production of taking careful notes on what he was wearing. She would then coax me into buying the same stylish materials, arrange some occasion to wear them, and just before we went out, would look me over and shake her head disconsolately. (I couldn't understand it either; I think she takes notes badly.)

And while there was no denying the stellar brilliance of the *Stage Door* cast, the ultimate success of the picture belonged to Greg La Cava. It unfortunately followed that Greg's success was attributable to his drinking which, sadly, had not changed since we made *My Man Godfrey*. Once again, this led to some painfully embarrassing moments, but from that same Muse who often caused him to fumble for names and stumble into furniture, came moments of sheer comedic genius, hundreds of them, all of which were conceived on the spot, and as a result of that improvisational crackle, *Stage Door* was imbued with a vitality that, in my opinion, hasn't diminished one iota in the near half-century since it was made.

In hopes that the La Cava-Ryskind winning streak would become three for three, Pan Berman asked us to take on *Room Service* with the Marx Brothers. It's pretty interesting to contemplate what might have resulted from a La Cava-Marx Brothers pairing, but it was not to be. Realizing that he had reached a now or never point, Greg dropped out of the project and spent the next two years coming to grips with his drinking problem. I was sorry to miss out on working with him again, especially with the potential that this project offered, but for Greg's sake I was happy that he was finally making the effort. And as for *Room Service*, I seriously doubt that even Greg's formidable talents could have saved it from being a misfire.

Aside from the fact that the original play wasn't a musical and that it wasn't written specifically for the Marx Brothers, both of which were dangerous deviations from the formula that had given the boys their past successes, the biggest problem that I had to contend with was the one of the setting. Ninety percent of the story was taken up with Groucho's stalling tactics to avoid being evicted from his hotel room. A theatrical audience will accept a story that takes place in one setting; in fact, fewer settings usually enhance a play's charm by shifting the emphasis toward the quality of the dialogue. But with movies tending to be primarily a visual medium, a one-set story can seem claustrophobic before the end of the first reel.

The problem of setting wasn't lost on the RKO hierarchy, but then again, neither was the fact that they had shelled out $225,000 for the film rights to *Room Service*. It was the largest single expenditure that the studio had ever made, and with an outlay of that size at stake, they weren't anxious to tamper with a proven success as we had done with *Stage Door*. *Room Service* had been a smash on Broadway; it was to be transferred intact (with a subsequent success) to the screen.

Well, RKO got a success out of *Room Service*, but unfortunately it wasn't with our version. There were a lot of funny moments in our effort, but on the whole it was a cramped, badly paced miscalculation that was dismissed by the critics and ignored by the public, which gives me the distinction of having written the best and the worst of the Marx Brothers movies. (I am, if nothing else, at least versatile.) During the war, RKO turned *Room Service* into the musical *Step Lively* with Frank Sinatra and George Murphy. The story was expanded beyond the one room, the musical numbers were properly integrated into the continuity, and the result was as entertaining as ours wasn't.

Of course, if one would only take the trouble to look, there are good points to be found in every endeavor, and it didn't take much looking to determine that Lucille Ball was the best thing about *Room Service*. This was Miss Ball's first starring role, and I do take some pride in knowing that I was able to help make that possible.

When we were making *Stage Door*, Miss Ball was a $50 a week contract player for RKO. She was assigned to the picture, but in the original version her part wasn't much more than a walk-on. While we were making the film, all the girls would gather their chairs into a circle for a gabfest between scenes. My chair was close to their bailiwick, and a lot of anecdotes that emanated from their sessions ended up in the script. But what really impressed me was Miss Ball's voice. There was just something very pleasant about the way it fell on my ears, and on the basis of that attraction I went to great lengths to build up her part. Greg agreed with my intentions, and he also went to some lengths to showcase Miss Ball's ability. When Greg was casting *Room Service*, he gave Miss Ball the lead, and the RKO chieftains stayed with his choice after Greg left the project. It was a wise decision, but it was followed by a boner. With her star on the rise, Miss Ball deservedly asked for a higher salary and was promptly dropped by the studio. I guess you could say that she exacted a somewhat classic revenge. After striking the "I Love Lucy" motherlode, Miss Ball bought RKO.

Between *Stage Door* and *Room Service* I had the opportunity of working with Miss Ball on *Having a Wonderful Time*. This was based on Arthur Kober's play about some Jewish girls going to summer camp. At that time Jews didn't exist in the movies, so all ethnic references were cut out of the script. This pretty much eliminated the threads that held the story together, but no one seemed to notice this until the filming was completed.

I was asked to come in and have a go at the project. After working on it for a while it seemed to me that reworking just a few crucial scenes would keep the story on track. I did the rewrites, and they brought in George Stevens to direct them. This also produced a pact for full collaboration, and this was the genesis of *Penny Serenade*.

At that time, George was best known for his work with Laurel and Hardy and Astaire and Rogers. Add to this my own outings with musicals and the Marxes, and it would not seem to be the sort of creative nucleus one normally associates with kitchen-sink-melodrama. Although we were clearly out of our element, there were some powerful inducements working on us to be there—Hitler for one. Europe had fallen to him, and England was holding on by her teeth. In the face of this, George wanted to tell a simple story that would be a reaffirmation of basic human dignity. We worked very closely together on that film, and I take a great deal of pride in the way it holds up to this day.

The success of *Penny Serenade* brought with it several offers to continue working under the dramatic mask, but I elected to stay on the lighter side of the lines. Some choice opportunities were forfeited by that decision—working with Sam Wood on *For Whom the Bell Tolls* for one—but in doing so, I was able to acquire some equally memorable experiences—working with Fred Allen definitely being one of them.

Here again I'm afraid I'm dropping a name that will be meaningless to the Beatles' generation, but for those of us who can remember when radio could boast of weekly shows that starred the comedic talents of Bob Hope, Eddie Cantor, Fanny Brice, Jack Benny, Burns and Allen, Groucho Marx, Ed Wynn, and Edgar Bergen, the curmudgeonly Fred Allen was, at least in my opinion, the best that the medium had to offer.

Considering the degree of talent represented by Allen's peerage, I realize that it's an exercise in recklessness to single out one of them as "best," but it seems to me that Allen does merit the distinction based on the fact that, unlike his contemporaries, Allen wrote most of his own material. For almost twenty years, especially during the days of "Allen's Alley," Allen's humor was an American institution, and even now, nearly thirty years after his passing, the intervals are very brief when I don't see one of his quotes prefacing an article, editorial, or book review.

It was the pressure of trying to top himself every week that brought Allen to my house. It's a matter of record that he was able to produce such a brilliant output, but it's been largely forgotten that it was done at the expense of a series of ulcers and coronaries. He was having an especially hard time of it in 1944, which resulted in his doctor ordering him to take a hiatus from the show. Allen was too restless a man to sit still for very long, and since the doctor had made no mention of the movies, it was only a matter of weeks before he arrived in Hollywood with a storyline that he had written with some writers in New York. He asked Jack Benny to recommend someone to help him with screenplay, and a few days later we were in business.

It took about two months for Allen and me to get *It's in the Bag* ready for filming. The writing was done at my house, and like myself, Allen was an incurable pacer. We started off in the upstair study, which is well suited to the pacings of one writer. With two of us in there, it only took about thirty seconds before we started to resemble a Groucho and Harpo routine. Thereafter, we relegated our enterprise to the living room as that area afforded us the longest stretch of uninterrupted ambulation.

When we finished with our two months of pacing, my wife needed a new carpet and Allen had a script in which he was to play the manager of a flea circus who was involved in a frantic attempt to retrieve a fortune in jewels that had been hidden in the false bottom of an inherited set of chairs. We were both pleased with the final draft, but when the picture was released, I'll have to allow that I was somewhat surprised by its success. Allen was the producer, and it seemed to me that he had created quite an obstacle for himself by casting William Bendix as his co-star. Bendix was a terrific actor, but an audience wants—expects—their pictures to be visually entertaining, and the combination of Allen and Bendix

surely had to be the most dour-looking duo in the history
of comedy.

At the completion of *It's in the Bag*, I had been working steadily as a writer on Broadway and in Hollywood
for twenty years. True enough, writers don't tote many
barges or lift many bales, but the profession is wrought
with a great many other debilitating perils. Twenty years
of blank pages and deadlines, producers' interferences
and actors' demands, out-of-town tryouts and opening-
night jitters, cancelled projects and emergency on-the-set
rewrites, middle-of-the-night inspirations and morning-
after despair, exhaustion, euphoria, burnout, and bliss—
all this, coupled with a nicotine and caffeine addiction
that could have given the shakes to a brontosaurus rex—
caught up with me around VJ Day. I had an ulcer. Boy,
did I have an ulcer, and not just the run-of-the-mill sour
stomach kind, mind you, but one so advanced that even
cottage cheese could set my esophagus on fire. I was
ordered to take a long rest and placed on a diet of such
unimaginable blandness that within a week I was prefer-
ring the illness to the cure. Thanks to my wife's diligence,
though, I was able to stick to it, and in about six months
I felt well enough to dust off the typewriter.

The assignment that Zeppo had waiting for me was to
transpose the French film *Battement de Coeur* into *Heartbeat* for RKO. Sam Wood was the director, and Ginger
Rogers and Adolph Menjou were the stars. The combination of those ingredients—my favorite studio and three of
my favorite people—made working on the project seem
almost as if it were a reward for having survived an
ordeal.

The storyline of the script that I was given was taken
up with the relationship of a Parisian gamine and the
diplomat that she was trained to pickpocket. It was an
interesting premise, but it had been written with a heavy
dollop of what I would call European pre-war cynicism.
Since our audience was to be post-war America where the
future held a great deal of promise, I turned everything

around accordingly. A few critics took exception to this, but each time that I've seen *Heartbeat* since then, I'm even more convinced of its effectiveness as a light entertainment.

Although I remain adamantly convinced that my creative contribution to *Heartbeat* was right on the money, there is no question that my participation in the project was a tremendous mistake. I had returned to work too soon, and this brought back my ulcer with a vengeance that landed me on a surgical table. The operation was deemed a success, but I was ordered not to work for an entire year. I complied, but as things turned out, the doctor need not have placed a time limit on my convalescence. My career in Hollywood had come to an abrupt halt with *Heartbeat*.

CHAPTER EIGHT

Whenever I was stymied by the topsy turvy world of the twenties, thirties, and forties, I could always take comfort in the knowledge that I could write a complaining article about those worries for *The Nation* and that would set the matter straight. There were times, I must confess, when I had my doubts as to whether or not *The Nation* actually did speak for the nation, but as one who took little solace in drink and even less in psychoanalysis, it became a case of taking one's comfort wherever it could be found.

The most invocative piece that I wrote for that venerable albeit portside publication was probably "No Soapboxes in Hollywood." This was in response to the lack of political awareness that I found in the film community after taking up residence there. In New York, you could always stop at "21" where Heywood Broun or Morris Ernst would be waxing discursive about what had appeared in that day's editorial pages. In Hollywood, any conversations to be encountered at the Trocadero or Musso & Franks were usually inspired by *Daily Variety*. There was activism in Hollywood at that time, quite a bit of it really, but it was to be some time before it became apparent that Hollywood's turmoils were part of a much, much larger political movement.

Nineteen-thirty-three was the year that saw Hollywood finally come to grips with a major problem that the studio executives had successfully managed to avoid since the film industry had been founded there twenty years earlier. When FDR closed the banks on March 8 of that year, in hopes of stopping a run on the widescale financial hoarding that was taking place, Hollywood, which had borrowed heavily to restructure itself for sound pictures suddenly found that it was unable to obtain any further credit. An emergency meeting was called of the industry's executives, and the following day every studio announced that any employee earning over $50 a week would be required to take a 50 percent cut in salary until the crisis was over.

Being that the electricians, engineers, grips, and musicians unions were protected by the International Alliance of Theatrical Stage Employees—IATSE—(prepare yourself as this is to be the first of many acronyms to follow) the brunt of the 50 percent cuts were taken by the "talent factions" that the studios held under contract: writers, actors, and directors. With no other option open to them, the "talent faction," the creative heart and soul of the film industry, tried to make the sacrifice as stoically as possible until full pay was eventually restored. (Only Sam Goldwyn made good on his promise of paying back the salaries that had been forfeited.) After all, those were very hard times and most people considered themselves lucky to have a job. The incident might well have been forgotten without a backward glance had it not been noticed during this time that MGM delivered the highest dividend its stockholders had received in quite some time. It was also very noticeable that none of the studio heads, Mayer, Thalberg, the brothers Warner, Harry Cohn, Carl Laemmle et al, felt it was necessary to set an example by cutting their own salaries in half. The combination of these two circumstances had the galvanizing effect of Marie Antoinette's fatal flippancy, and from this came Hollywood's version of the storming of the Bastille—unionism.

A great deal of the labor tension that had been fomenting in Hollywood up to that time had been deftly neutralized by the creation of the Academy of Motion Picture Arts and Sciences. In its original concept, the Academy was designed not only to dispense its annual awards, but also to function as arbitrator between the industry's executives and employees. There were branches for writers, actors, and directors, which made it look good in concept, but with the academy completely controlled by the studio executives, its ability to govern impartially seemed reminiscent of the power days of Tammany Hall.

Another thought which I still believe will find currency is that it was to the great credit of Hollywood's writers that they were the first to challenge the inequity of the academy's domination by formally establishing the Screen Writers Guild on 6 April 1933. Although this was to send chills through Hollywood's corporate spine, the SWG's proposals seem in retrospect to be as modest as they were justified: (a) the guild be recognized as the sole bargaining representative of the industry's writers; (b) a minimum wage be established; and (c) the guild would have the power of arbitration in matters of screen credits.

This last objective was perhaps more important than the combination of the other two. In the early years of the academy's existence, one of its bylaws stated that the producer on any given picture would have the power of determining the writing credit. It would seem that in films, as in politics, absolute power tends to corrupt, which accounted for the widescale practice of the producers and directors—especially in silent pictures—claiming the credit for themselves while the poor souls that actually sweated out the process of turning blank pages into a workable script would quite often receive nothing for their efforts but a salary. Aside from the fact that writers' contracts were renegotiated on the basis of accumulated credits—no credits, no salary adjustments—this practice brought into question the larger ethical issue of separating a writer from his creation, and as any writer will corroborate, this is the unkindest cut of all.

Seeking to halt this literary piracy by founding the SWG was a very bold step to be taken in the face of some potentially ruinous opposition, as subsequent events were to prove. Initially, however, the founding of the guild turned out to be neither the panacea that its members had hoped for, nor the donnybrook that they had expected. It didn't accomplish much of anything really. The power still lay in the hands of the producers and their only acknowledgment of the fledgling organization was one of the benign contempt.

Despite the studio heads' indifference—and, in many cases, because of it—the SWG membership continued to grow over the next two years into a force of over five hundred. These were numbers which couldn't be ignored, and in hopes of placating this new threat that had sprung up in their midst, the executives made some changes in the bylaws of the writers branch of the academy. This was a blatant case of tokenism and it backfired on them in a big way. Hundreds of SWG members resigned from the academy, and in one of the most celebrated moments of the SWG's stormy chronicles, Dudley Nichols, in a pique of eloquent rebuttal, refused to accept his Best Screenplay Oscar for *The Informer*. After being stung by this effrontery, the producers started playing hard ball with a vengeance that made it impossible to work in Hollywood and remain neutral on the issue of unionism.

It happened at this time that I was working on *My Man Godfrey* at Universal. One afternoon while I was sitting in my office desperately trying to rewrite a scene that was to be filmed as soon as I could finish it—the studio operator—apparently due to the similarity of our last names—put a call through to me that was meant for Allen Rivken. The caller, a highly placed officer at MGM, became one of the dark figures of the Hollywood civil war by intimidating the industry's junior writers one of whom Rivken happened to be at that time. Before realizing that he had reached the wrong party, I received an icy earful about how Rivken would be well advised to get out of the SWG if he wanted to continue working in the business. I'm not a joiner by nature, but I have no stomach for that kind of intimidation. Pushed off the fence as it were, I landed in the ranks of SWG upstarts where, I had no sooner stood up to be counted, than I found myself becoming the recipient of some strong arm tactics that were most decidedly meant for me.

The trouble began in the wake of the Dudley Nichols snub, when the negotiations between the SWG and the producers turned bitter and then broke down completely. Frustrated by yet another stalemate, the executive board of the guild proposed to strengthen our bargaining position by calling for an amalgamation between the SWG and the powerful resources of the New York-based Authors League of America (ALA). It was calculated that if nothing else, this would at least help to reopen some sorely needed communication between the two parties. Unfortunately, this was only to prove that the guild was just as capable of tactical blunders as the producers, perhaps even more so as this backfired in our faces in the worst of all possible ways: it brought Irving Thalberg into the fracas.

Although our brief relationship that I had established with Irving Thalberg during the making of *A Night at the Opera* wasn't what I would consider to be a cordial one, it was, I feel correct in stating, based on a mutual respect. Probably the most notable manifestation of this was that he never forced me to wait (as he was legendary for doing) on the "million dollar bench" of his outer office where a number of the most highly priced writers, actors, and directors in the business often spent hours waiting for the great man to vouchsafe them an audience. I always had an easy access to him and I must say that it was something of a heady experience to be waved straight through to his office while all of those million dollar eyes were shooting million dollar daggers into my back.

Thalberg had been strongly opposed to the SWG since its formation. Being that his borealis was indisputably the brightest in the Hollywood firmament at the time, his decision to ignore the guild's existence ruled as the governing strategy of his fellow producers until the ALA amalgamation was proposed. The day before the scheduled vote on the merger, 1 May 1936 to be exact, that silence was broken. Thalberg called for a meeting of the Producers Association in the MGM screening room, during which he spelled out for them an apocryphal vista of what was no longer an industry wage dispute, but a most certain loss of their control to an outside concern. Apparently it was a successful sell, because the next day meetings were held between management and the writers at every studio in town.

At that time, fate had me finishing up *My Man Godfrey* which showed every indication of being as big a success as *A Night at the Opera* had been. With two back-to-back hits to my credit, Zeppo was able to convince the executives at Universal that I had the natural born ability to be a producer. He had a somewhat harder time of it convincing me. I had spent my entire life honing my ability to sit at a typewriter and produce dialogue which might, in some small way, help ease mankind's burdens through laughter. I felt that it was a noble calling and being that it was the only endeavor in life that I could perform with any degree of proficiency, it seemed to me that my talent must have had some sort of divine direction behind it. And on the note of aesthetic purity, I turned down the offer. Zeppo said that as a producer I could double my salary, and I said that I would give it a try.

Try it I did, but my dreams of moguldom—the beach house for my wife, the European finishing schools for my kids, and the yacht which would give me status (and, undoubtedly, sea sickness)—were to be short-lived. At the May 1 showdown meeting between Universal's writers and executives, William Keonig, one of the studio's higher officers, passed around pledges to each of the writers asking us to vote against the amalgamation. Apparently hoping to capitalize on my impending elevation to the rank of producer, Mr. Keonig called on me unexpectedly to voice my disapproval of the merger. (I didn't appreciate being put on the spot in that manner, but even if I had known of his intentions, producer's contract or not, I considered myself first and foremost to be a writer.) When I said this as a prelude to announcing my intention to vote for the affiliation, I suddenly became a hero to the studio's writers and a pariah to its executives. Two days later, Zeppo called with the news that my contract wouldn't be going through because of the stance I had taken at the meeting. I said that would be fine with me because if those good fellows at the Universal were going to adopt that sort of attitude then I would just as soon not be in their employment. (The actual wording of my response might have been a tad stronger than that, but I'm striving so hard to keep this remembrance on a gentlemanly level.)

Two days after that exchange, Zeppo called with news that my contract had been approved and was awaiting my signature. To this day, I don't know how he did it, what strings he pulled, what punches he threw, or what buried bodies he threatened to uncover. Whenever I would press him on the matter, he would merely smile and fend me off with an airy, "Just trust me." Which I did.

Trusting Zep on this matter required an extra measure of faith, especially when I learned that before I became a producer, I would first have to work as an associate producer which required that I take a considerable cut in the salary that I was earning as a writer. I was none too pleased with that arrangement, but as Zeppo ever so patiently explained to me in A-B-C terms, advancing within the studio's power structure was somewhat similar to playing the children's game of "Mother May I?"—one had to take a half step backward in order to take two giant steps forward. The whole business was too Byzantine for me to follow, but if anyone in Hollywood

knew which side of the butter his bread clings to, it was
Zep. So, with my family's welfare in his hands, I switched
careers.

When I told my wife that I had been promoted/
demoted to associate producer, she said "Congratulations, but what's an associate producer?" It's a question
I'll warrant is asked of everyone who has ever held the
job. Theoretically the position was created to act as a
liaison between the producer and the director. Depending on the *modus operandi* of any given producer or director, an AP's duties can range from heavy involvement to
casual association, the latter being especially true in cases
of nepotism. One of the more famous examples was the
time an exasperated producer succumbed to family pressure and hired an inept in-law for the position, but only
after inserting a clause into the contract stipulating that
he was never to set foot on the studio lot while the film
was being made.

The first assignment that I worked on in my new
capacity was a Jane Wyatt-Louis Hayward-Eugene Pallette
comedy titled *The Luckiest Girl in the World*. I was given
a small office equipped with a chair, a desk, and a moun-
tainous stack of paperwork that ranged from approving
the costs of material for the wardrobe department, to
projecting the carpenter's overtime. Just like every other
businessman in the country I worked very diligently in
my office from nine until six, and after about a week of
that the name Zeppo was never to roll off my tongue
without an invective preceding it. Unfulfilling though it
was, I did stick with it, and the picture turned out well,
and as Zeppo had promised, I was given the permission
to take my two giant steps forward.

Although I had insisted that Universal strike the anti-
guild provisions from my contract before I would sign on
as an associate producer, and while my commitment to
the SWG hadn't waned while I was serving in that function, Universal paid no heed whatsoever to my pro-guild
sentiments when it came time for me to sign my new

contract as a producer. This was mainly due to the fact that the guild had ceased to exist. The producers had crushed it by suggesting that remaining in the SWG would be synonymous with a terminated contract when options time came around. It was a suggestion which very few in the guild failed to heed.

It was during this time that the guild was being eradicated that communism first became a focal point of contention in Hollywood. This was to produce a rift within the writing community that was even more bitter than the one between the SWG and the producers, and judging from public television's annual diatribe against the faction that I ultimately sided with, the issue still seems as misunderstood today as it was then.

When the Screen Writers Guild was founded in 1933, it had eight charter members. Through a Dickensian twist of fate, the polarization that was about to overtake our merry little band of writers during that disjunctive summer of 1936 was spearheaded by two of those founders; John Howard Lawson and John Lee Mahin. Lawson, who was elected the first president of the guild came to be openly acknowledged as the "commissar" of the Communist party in Hollywood. Mahin, who left the guild because of the CP's attempt at radicalizing it, was elected as the first president of the Screen Playwrights (SP), an organization of writers which he and his fellow MGM writer James Kevin McGuiness had established as an alternative union that would be free of the influence of communism. They presented their charter to Irving Thalberg who grudgingly recognized them as the lesser of two evils, and the fireworks began.

At the time they were forming the Screen Playwrights, John Lee Mahin and Jim McGuiness, both of whom I considered to be close friends, made quite an effort to get me to sign up with their group. While I was in complete agreement with them on the necessity of countering the growing Communist threat, I felt that the best way to go about it would be to stay and fight from within the guild. They disagreed, arguing that the Communists were already too deeply entrenched there for us to have any effect. Try though we did, we could never come to terms which regrettably led to a precipitous cooling off of our friendships.

While it bothered me greatly to be at odds with a group of men for whom I had such respect, I felt (and still do) that I had the greater reason to be disappointed with them than they had with me. For having made membership to the SP contingent upon having written three screenplays in two years, they were in effect saying "the hell with the younger writers." It was an attitude which smacked of elitism, and being that it was on behalf of the junior writers that the movement for representation had been started (and certainly no one knew this better than John Lee Mahin) it therefore became inevitable that the up and comers would turn resentful when the SP—which had the outward appearance of being comprised of the industry's higher paid writers—suddenly turned their backs on those who were still struggling. The Communists immediately set about turning that resentment to their advantage, and it's been one of the major regrets of my life that I was unable to convince such SP stalwarts as Mahin, McGuiness, and Herman Mankiewicz that their abrasive tactics were making that opportunity possible.

My reservations about the SP meant very little when stacked up against Irving Thalberg's endorsement which was tantamount to being the keys to the kingdom. Within a week of the SP's formation, their "flying squadron"—Mahin and McGuiness along with Pat McNutt and Howard Emmett Rogers—were pressing their case for membership before mandatory assemblages of writers at every studio in town. The SWG clearly had the best interests of the writers at heart, but what could we offer to a writer but an uncertain future while membership in the SP was being rewarded with the coveted long term contract? Accordingly, there were less than one hundred of us left in the guild by September while the SP's enrollment had risen to nearly five hundred. In light of those circumstances it was senseless to carry on the fight, good one that it was, so we simply cancelled our charter and went back to work.

With the wars over—or so I thought—the credit:

Produced by
Morrie Ryskind

became a reality. I have to admit that I'm rather fond of the way that reads, but alas, this page is the only place where it has ever had a practical application. The picture that was assigned to me was the project which took me to New Orleans where I encountered the incident that I was subsequently able to turn into *Louisiana Purchase*. When I returned to Hollywood, a combination of trouble with the script, the unavailability of a star that we had hoped to get, and the unexpected release of a similar movie by another studio resulted in my project being shelved. While I was starting to prepare another project, a spark flamed up from the SWG ashes, and in less time than it would have taken Jerusalem Slim and the Wobblies to warble through a chorus of "Hallelujah, I'm a bum," unionism was once again a red-hot issue in Hollywood.

By way of background information, I should point out that the SWG has been founded under the auspices of FDR's National Recovery Act (NRA)—believe me, I'm just as weary of these acronyms as you are, but please bear with me for just a little while longer. Unfortunately, as with so many of the New Deal measures which failed to make utopia utope, the NRA didn't work out and was struck down by the Supreme Court for being unconstitutional. Fortunately though, its provisions on labor were incorporated into the Wagner Labor Act which Congress did pass in July of 1935. This declared unequivocally that collective bargaining was the official policy of the United States, and that should have been that.

Unfortunately (again), no sooner had the Wagner Act been passed than its legality was subjected to a constitutional challenge by a disgruntled Eastern corporation which tied it up in the courts for two years and gave the producers in Hollywood a legal excuse for not honoring it. Fortunately (again), that excuse was invalidated on 12 April 1937 when the Supreme Court declared that the Wagner Act was indeed constitutional and should be implemented forthwith. The Hollywood grapevine was renowned for its speed, but that particular hosanna was to move along it at a faster clip than anything I ever observed. Everywhere, writers were collecting in small groups, and everywhere, the whispered question was the same: "If this brings back the guild, are you going to join?"

When the questioning got around to me, I replied that "yes" I would rejoin if the guild got back on its feet. I wasn't militant about it, then or ever, but I saw no reason why a man should have to be clandestine about his union affiliation, especially in a year which celebrated the 150th anniversary of our constitution. The executives to whom I reported at Universal saw it differently however, and once again I found myself becoming *persona non grata* there. My appointments to go in and see them about production details were repeatedly cancelled, my phone calls weren't returned and after about a week of that I said, "enough already" and asked Zeppo to get me out of my contract. Universal seemed only too happy to oblige, and I was only too happy to trundle off to RKO where I caught up with Greg La Cava.

There were many aspects about returning to the guild that I was somewhat less than thrilled with. The tenuousness of our relationship with the producers had necessitated that an element of cloak and dagger be used during the reorganization. The blacklisting tactics that had been used against us the previous summer were still very much on everyone's minds that spring. Not wanting to get bludgeoned two years running, it was decided that the wiser move would be to forgo having an open membership drive. Instead, a series of small meetings were held in the homes of several of the SWG's diehards. Each member would invite ten or fifteen prospective members, state our case, and ask them to join. Given that we were being followed and spied on by both the producers' hired detectives and the SP, all of that James Bond sort of business was our only hope for success. It all seemed very justifiable at the time but even still, having to do anything that required one to sneak around in the night in that manner also made it seem very distasteful to me.

The secrecy did work though, and by the eleventh of June when we rented the Hollywood Athletic Club to hold our first open meeting, the resurrected guild had over four hundred members. That night, Dudley Nichols was elected president, Charles Brackett the vice-president, Frances Goodrich as secretary, John Greg the treasurer, and Sheridan Gibney, Albert Hackett, Dashiel Hammett, Lillian Hellman, Brian Marlow, Edwin Justus Mayer, Jane Murfin, Dorothy Parker, Samson Raphaelson, Donald Ogden Stewart, and myself were elected to the executive board. As writers go, I thought we were a rather distinguished group; as administrators and managerial types, well, just let it be said that we were a distinguished group of writers.

As politics went, the anti-Red sentiments held by a few of us and the pro-Soviet sympathies held by a like number of the board members made us quite a disparate group. The divisiveness however wasn't a problem at first, as all factionalism was surrendered to the higher interests of the guild, such as its survival. In doing so, our immediate goal was to petition the National Labor Relations Board (NLRB), asking them to preside over an election which would determine whether the SWG or the SP would be the sole bargaining agency for film writers. The obstacle to this was whether or not screenwriters would qualify as laborers under the Wagner Act. The producers were arguing, quite vociferously as I recall, that writers were artists and therefore were not eligible for unionization. Our argument: "If we were artists and not laborers, then why did every studio's writer's building have a timeclock that all contract employees had to punch coming and going the way every worker did at Lockheed?" Naturally, we felt that our Solomonesque sagacity made for the stronger argument, but as there wasn't a precedent to go on, and as once again the producers had rolled out their threats of blacklisting, waiting for the NLRB's decision about accepting our petition was a very anxious period for most of the SWG membership.

It was during this period that Rupert Hughes (uncle to the eccentric Howard of the Spruce Goose/billion dollar fortune fame) succeeded John Lee Mahin as president of the Screen Playwrights. Rupert was a feisty old bird, and he was no sooner in office than he tore into the SWG with a virulent series of "open letters" in the Hollywood trade papers. This was an obvious calculation on behalf of the SP to stave off potential SWG recruits, and, unfortunately, it was taking its effect. Something had to be done about it, and the only something that I could think of was to take out my own full-page response (as a private citizen and not on the guild's behalf) in the *Hollywood Reporter*.

In brief, my purpose was to state that I was not interested in biting producers, some of whom I considered to be good friends even though their horses were always costing me money, but I did feel it necessary to call to their attention—and to Rupert's—that totalitarianism was the governing force in Russia, Italy, and Germany at that time. I also felt compelled to bring up the fact that we were living in a democratic nation, and that one of the great bulwarks of a democracy was the principle of collective bargaining. Since I was certain that we were all in agreement that we didn't want what was happening in Europe to happen here, my question to Rupert was, "Why were the producers, with whom the SP was so closely aligned (a) refusing to meet with the representatives chosen by their employees, and (b) aggravating the situation even further with their threats of blacklisting?"

Other than the satisfaction that I felt at having written it, I doubt that my joust with Rupert accomplished very much. Secretly, I had been hoping that its effect would be somewhat along the lines of Prince Hal's call to arms at Agincourt, but apparently, epic grandeur was not in my cards.

One young "chutzpanik" whose contributions to the guild were invaluable, was Leonard Jaofsky. I doubt that today any active member of the WGA would recognize that name, but without his skill and dedication the guild would surely have been crushed in the legal onslaught that followed.

After accepting our petition, the NLRB scheduled advisory hearings to take place in Los Angeles that October. This opened up the possibility of a favorable SWG ruling and that immediately turned the proceedings into a David vs. Goliath struggle with worldwide press coverage being accorded to every detail. On the one side, slingshot at the ready, stood Janofsky, an attorney with the ability of Clarence Darrow and the eyebrows of Leonid Brezhnev, whom we had selected (after I had the privilege of nominating him) to represent the guild. Pitted against him were a platoon of attorneys representing: the Screen Playwrights, the Motion Picture Producers and Distributors Association, the Association of Motion Picture Producers and the production corporations of MGM, RKO, 20th Century-Fox, Selznick International, Walter Wagner, Universal, Republic, Goldwyn, Columbia, Armour, Walt Disney, Grand National, Hal Roach, and Monogram. As a member of the guild's board of directors, it was incumbent on me to attend some of those hearings. My usual enthusiasm for courtroom proceedings is on a par with root canal work, but in watching the crafty Janofsky repeatedly draw those opposing attorneys into a parlous ambuscade, I couldn't help but feel I had a ringside seat at the best show in town.

One incident which had the earmarks of high drama about it occurred on the day before the hearings closed.

The lawyers of the anti-SWG pact were hoping to use ridicule as the foundation of their closing argument by quoting the salaries (including mine) of several of the higher paid writers in the guild. Then, in a great rhetorical flourish they asked, "These are the people that need the protection of a union?" As legal maneuvers go, it was a very effective tactic, but Janofsky was able to turn it back on them by citing the overall grosses of the motion picture industry and then showing how little of it was being filtered down to the majority of writers who were making it possible. The attorneys for the Goliath faction violently objected to this, so much so that an exchange between Janofsky and the SP's lawyer ended with both men shucking off their jackets and preparing to duke it out. Fortunately, some swift moving bailiffs separated them and order was restored. After a cooling off period, Janofsky cited some recent decisions of the Supreme Court which allowed the gross incomes of corporations to be used in cases involving the Wagner Act. The judge upheld the precedent, and this pretty much cinched the case for the guild.

When the NLRB panel packed their briefcases and returned to Washington, the mood of the SWG was exultant. This was to prove transitory, because the wheels of labor resolutions are apparently synchronized with the wheels of justice. I don't wish to be disrespectful of either institution but to this day I still haven't the foggiest idea why it took nine entire months for the NLRB to announce a decision. This delay, as you might well imagine, made for a very uneasy interim in Hollywood. The rift between the SWG/S—membership grew more and more embittered during this time, and I was to witness and experience many a terminated friendship. The worst of it seemed to take place in the studio commissaries which, like ancient Gaul, were divided into three parts. There were tables for writers, actors, and directors, and befitting the industry's class structure, these distinctions were honored a great deal more scrupulously in the observance than in the breach. When the guild reorganized, the SP members extended this division even further by staking out their own tables. Now, the mere act of sitting down to lunch, after first negotiating a gauntlet of cold stares, became an act of allegiance to one of the disparate factions.

The commissary cold wars ended on the seventh of June (We're in 1938 now) when the NLRB finally announced that screenwriters most definitely were to be classified as employees (thus ended my days as an artist) under the specifications of the Wagner Act. This was good news, but the fact that we had only three weeks to prepare ourselves for a certification election which would legally establish which organization would have the power of representation wasn't. Because the guild could claim nearly 75 percent of the writers in Hollywood as members, we were at first ecstatic, but an NLRB small-print proviso stipulating that only those writers who were working as of June fourth would be eligible to vote threatened once again to throw our victory back into the jaws of defeat. Since the Screen Playwrights all had studio contracts, their entire membership automatically qualified, while the SWG, which had a large element of free-lancers who were between assignments suddenly didn't have the power base that we thought we did. Dudley Nichols called an emergency meeting of the board, and we set up a series of rallies to shore up our voting strength. The turnouts were very encouraging, but even with this effort, the arithmetic still wasn't in our favor going into the election.

Taking note of the great distances (often referred to as galactic) that separated the studios in Hollywood, the NLRB sought to insure maximum participation in the election by setting up three different polling centers—one in Burbank to cover the San Fernando Valley (Warner Brothers, Universal, Republic, et al), one in Culver City (MGM, 20th Century-Fox, Hal Roach, etc.), and one at the Roosevelt Hotel on Hollywood Boulevard where Paul

Jarrico and I served as the SWG's precinct wardens. Say what you will about the NLRB's laggardly process of making decisions, but their choice of the Roosevelt—a much frequented SWG watering hole due to its equidistance between Burbank and Culver City—won them many a friend in the guild that day. Almost the entire membership had converged there by the time we sealed the ballot boxes and sent them to the NLRB headquarters, and by eight o'clock, the encirclement of the bar into the Blossom Room was five deep.

Barring providential intervention, our main hope of winning rested on the NLRB's stipulation that the election be conducted by a secret vote. The producers, however, were lobbying for an open show of hands with the sort of fervor that was later to propel the Wehrmacht into Poland. Again, congratulations are due to the NLRB for not knuckling under to that pressure, for it was the protective anonymity of these secret ballots that gave us the day. Billy Wilder had been officiating as a SWG counter at the NLRB headquarters, and when he walked into the Roosevelt, his Cheshire grin said all that needed to be said. What he couldn't have said because of the uproar that followed, was that a sizable portion of those who were registered with the SP had crossed over to our side to give us a four-to-one margin. Now by nature I am not much of one for late-night carousing, but it was such a joyous relief to be finished with the whole ugly business that, I must confess, by the time I raised my final cup of amphora to the weal of our victorious guild, the rising sun had already gilded the MGM water tower and the merry kingdom of L. B. Mayer over which it lorded.

Even with the ill effects of the celebration caroming through my frazzled brain like Wagnerian thunder, I can remember thinking what a fine and wonderful place the world was that morning. However, with the arrival of the evening newspaper came the return of the old feeling that the SWG was forever to be synonymous with sackcloth and ashes. Having conceded nothing, the producers were: (a) insisting that their contract with the SP had not been nullified by the election, and (b) were threatening to press that argument all the way to the Supreme Court if necessary. Some nine months later (we're now into the spring of 1939), nine entire months while the guild was legally hamstrung, the opening salvo of that threat got underway.

When the NLRB convened the appeal hearings which the producers had demanded, I was one of several witnesses that Leonard Janofsky summoned to the stand on behalf of the guild. The representatives for the producers were professing a total ignorance about the guild ever receiving anything but total cooperation and encouragement from them, and Janofsky sought to refute this by having me recount the incidents that occurred at Universal during the time of the ALA amalgamation. When I had made my statement, the attorney for the SP tried to turn the issue to their advantage by bringing up the question of arbitration. "Isn't it true that when you signed the contract, you compelled the producers to eliminate a clause referring all questions of arbitration to the Screen Playwrights?" When I answered that this was true, Janofsky was able to turn the tables on them once again by interposing, "But isn't it true that you are such a skilled and high priced scenario writer that you were able to compel the producers to do this because they needed your services?" Before I could speak, the panoply of attorneys that opposed Janofsky objected to the question in outraged unison. Although the objection was sustained and the question ordered stricken from the transcript, the alacrity with which they sprang to Janofsky's bait made a telling statement to the Labor Board about the inequity of the arbitration system. This maneuver, I am told, is a very old trick in legal circles.

To no one's surprise, that second round of NLRB hearings ended in the same manner as the first session: the lawyers packed their briefcases and returned to Washington and everyone in Hollywood settled in for several months of second-guessing the outcome. There was a major extortion scandal involving payoffs between the producers and several IATSE officials during this time and rumors were then rife about the NLRB payoffs taking place in Washington. We had suffered too many last-minute reversals not to take them seriously and had they proved to be true, the emotional impact on the collectively frayed nerves of the guild would probably have been sufficient to prevent us from effectively reorganizing.

Having taken our usual precaution of preparing for the worst, the NLRB's announcement that the SWG certification was to be upheld came, with somewhat melodramatic flair, just in time to give everyone in the guild an unexpected note of good cheer for the holiday season. A cautious note of good cheer, I should add, since no one really expected much to come out of the NLRB's directive even though the producers were warned that failure to comply would result in criminal charges being filed against them. Nothing did come of it for several weeks other than a strong silence, but shortly after the New Year (we're now in 1940), the pall cast over the nation by the outbreak of war in Europe highlighted the need for unity at home and with that pressure weighing on them, the Producers Association announced that there would be no further legal challenges against the sovereignty of the Screen Writers Guild.

So, it was over. Well, almost. The ensuing negotiations lasted for fifteen months before a final accord was reached (and might still be going on had we not threatened to strike), but on 18 June 1941, over nine years after it was founded, the Screen Writers Guild signed its first contract. The agreement, which was effective for seven years, gave us an 85 percent guild shop for three years, upgraded to 90 percent thereafter, a minimum pay scale of $125 a week for all writers including those who wrote short subjects, and most important, arbitration of screen credits were now to be controlled by the guild.

Considering the odds that had to be overcome, the actual working implementation of the guild represented quite an achievement in the field of labor relations. The Writers Guild of America is still operating under the basic framework of the 1941 contract, and I'm proud that I was able to play a part in having made it possible.

I wish that I could report that between 1937 and 1947 my commitment to the establishment of the Screen Writers Guild—in terms of time, energy, and money—equaled that of any other person of Hollywood, but this was not the case. The top honors for an unswerving SWG commitment rightfully belong to that bloc in our midst who hoped to use the guild as the power base that would enable them to bring all facets of the motion picture industry under the control of one all-encompassing super union which would be controlled by and serve the purposes of the Communist party. And there, to glom a phrase from the melancholy Prince of Denmark, was the rub.

At this point of my life, it is a rub that I am content to leave alone. There has been a mountain of material written about the communism issue in Hollywood, none of which doesn't set my teeth on edge, as well as a number of similarly-themed PBS documentaries (diatribes would be the better word), none of which hasn't left me thundering philippics and jeremiads for several hours. If I've digested those liberal-slanted offerings correctly, and goodness knows that I've tried, their thesis holds that the only people in Hollywood who belong to the Communist party were those that were fabricated in the febrile paranoia of flag-waving yahoos such as myself. To these would-be Zolas—especially the gang at PBS—I can only say that your depiction of those polarizing events differs drastically from the way that I remember it.

To fully detail that turbulent period would detail writing a book. Anything less would be a disservice to both sides, and for that reason I'm going to beg off the subject, content in the knowledge that Roy Brewer is

finally at work on his long promised volume. Roy, whom
I've been proud to claim as one of my closest friends for
the past forty years, was head of Hollywood's trade unions
during the height of the communism fight. Roy's position
gave him an almost equal standing with the studio heads
whose gross negligence about hiring Communists is what
made the whole ugly mess inevitable. Probably more so
than any other one person that I know of, Roy helped
bring the situation under control. When Roy flexed his
muscle, the producers had to take notice, and I think this
nation owes Roy one hell of a big note of thanks.

As for my own part in that long controversy, I'll only
say that I did not think anyone who was subscribing to
the tenets of the Communist party should be allowed to
work in positions where they might influence the content
of motion pictures. I was never hesitant about expressing
that sentiment, the result of which found me being sub-
poenaed to testify against the infamous "Hollywood Ten."

In my incautious youth, I was known to protest against
the executions of Sacco and Vanzetti, circulate petitions
on behalf of the Scottsboro boys, and help raise money
for the defense fund of Tom Mooney's retrial. Had the
Hollywood Ten been advocating voodooism, blank verse,
or a return to the silver standard, I would have defended
their right to privacy of association. But when it came to
their support—their very active support—of a political party
which had, as its stated objective, the overthrow of the
American constitutional form of government, I couldn't
help but look on them as agents of a foreign power, nor
could I keep myself from thinking that they got off rather
lightly by just being blacklisted.

Such sentiments, I'm sure, will chill many a heart in
liberal circles. Should any of that faction still be reading,
you may take some comfort in knowing that my heresy
did not go unpunished. For, you see, there was another—
a grey list, if you will—to come out of those 1947 congressional hearings, and my name was on it.

In his autobiography *Take Two*, Phillip Dunne of the

loyal opposition specifically mentions my name to express his doubt that Hollywood's power elite instituted a reverse sort of blacklist against those of us in the MPA who were responsible for the industry's dirty linen being washed in public. (The MPA was the Motion Picture Alliance for the Preservation of American Ideals, and the title was, I concede, grandiose.) Well, I've admired Phil Dunne for over fifty years, as a man, as a writer, and—I hope this doesn't jeopardize his standing in the liberal community—as a friend, although I can't say that I was overly pleased with his depiction of me as "one of the most garrulous witnesses" to take the stand against the Hollywood Ten.

While I have a great respect for Phil's integrity, it seems to me that on this one score about the blacklist he was wrong. I can't completely discount his contention, because there is a chance that the shut-out status that befell a few of us was a coincidence. However, what tends to put me off the coincidence theory is the memory of that meeting in Jim McGuiness' office at MGM. On the day before we were scheduled to take the train to Washington, Jim called and asked me to come over right away. John Charles Moffit and Fred Niblo Jr. (MPA members, as was Jim) were already there along with two attorneys from the Producers Association. As the four of us were writers and would be testifying about the way the Communists had infiltrated the SWG, the lawyers had asked for the meeting to request that we soften our testimony. They argued that the MPA had already done enough damage to the prestige of the industry by sending the delegation to Washington which resulted in the hearings being convened and that it would serve no purpose to add further fuel to fire. We replied that since we would be under oath, there wouldn't be any way that we could take any evasions. When their reiterated plea was met by the same answer, the attorneys stormed out of Jim's office with a parting growl about the industry knowing how to protect itself. To my mind that constituted a threat.

In the twelve years prior to my testimony at the 1947 HUAC hearings at Washington, I was consistently one of the ten highest paid writers in Hollywood. I turned down, on the average, at least three assignments for every one that I accepted, and I feel safe in saying that I was welcome at every studio in town. After I testified against the Hollywood Ten, I was never again to receive one single offer from any studio, and the same fate befell McGuiness, Niblo, and Moffit, all of whom had credentials that matched mine. Here again, I can only state that this might well have been a coincidence—life's full of them. But if that were indeed the case, then I would like to nominate our circumstances for the coincidence of the century.

That being stated, I wish to go no further into that matter. To do so, I would have to wrap myself in a cloak of martyrdom, and that is a thought which I refuse to entertain. But for the record, I would like it known that if I had it all to do over again, aided by nearly forty years of hindsight, I would respond no differently on the issue of communism in Hollywood than I did then.

CHAPTER NINE

I remain, I strongly suspect, the only person of either (or no) sex who has written a Broadway show or a Hollywood scenario and has never been psychoanalyzed. This has made me something of an oddity in Hollywood, at least in the eyes of all the neighboring parents who shriek "Unclean!" and whisk their children from my path. Now, I crave affection as much as the next fellow, but I remain adamant about avoiding that Procrustean couch—not so much out of a disbelief in Dr. Freud's theories, as in the belief that writers should be paid for what's in their heads, and that a dangerous precedent is being set whenever that process is reversed. As psychoanalysis remains to this day one of Hollywood's most celebrated social franchises, that notion was never to find popular support. This I can attest to from the nearly fifty years of dinner parties that I have either hosted or attended, all of which, alas, were inevitably ruined by at least one enlightened writer who insisted on going on about the aggressive tendencies and potty habits of his siblings—which, apparently, are what Freudians have instead of children.

The Hollywood vogue for the "Jewish science from Vienna," as Woody Allen so adroitly describes it, got underway during the thirties when a large influx of thickly accented (mostly German) doctors, whose credentials

ranged from genuine to quack, descended on our fair
cinematropolis. (So help me, there was once a Wilshire
Boulevard storefront window that proclaimed: HIGH
COLONICS AND PSYCHOANALYSIS $5.) Everyone, and
by the use of that all-inclusive term I can offer Chico
Marx as an illustration of its absurdest extremes, was
caught up in the Freudian allure. Thankfully, Groucho,
who would never submit himself to "Groucho on the
coucho" (his words), was around to keep Chico in perspective.

Chico's announcement that he was going to see one
of the good Herr doctors came at a time when dream
analysis, the train and the tunnel and that sort of thing,
had just become all the rage. It seem that poor Chico was
being bothered by a recurring vision in which he saw
himself as Quasimodo. When he made the mistake of
musing aloud, "I wonder what it means?" Groucho was
there to jump in with, "It probably means that you're too
old to be making love in the bathtub."

Although I still find this whole business of dream
analysis suspect, I must admit that for the past forty years
or so, I too have been host to a frequently recurring
dream. As dreams go, it's rather subdued, but nevertheless, it was a cherished source of revitalization to me
during all those years.

The subject of the enchanted vision is simply yours
truly ensconced before the TV set watching a public
affairs program on a Sunday afternoon. Now we've all
been through enough of those shows to know that when
the cognoscenti sit down to make an analysis of anything
as nebulous as public affairs, Gresham's law takes over
completely and the resulting analysis is even nebulousier
than the subject was to begin with. The most that one can
hope for is some interesting talk before the host sums
everything up because it's time to get off the air, and
some conclusions must be reached.

Now to the average person, the idea of being stuck
with this recurrence for forty years would probably sug-

gest nothing less than karmic retribution for an offense equal to those of the Borgias. Mine, however, remains a dream and not a nightmare by virtue of the topic being discussed by the panelists: Resolved, That Conservatism Would Be Of Far Greater Benefit To America Than Liberalism. What makes this such a sweet dream, and for most of the years I've had it, "The Impossible Dream," is the people who make up that panel. The cast has changed over the years, as has the medium from radio to TV, but in the latest manifestation they are: Mike Wallace, David Brinkley, John Chancellor, Eric Sevareid, Walter Cronkite, Dan Rather, Katharine Graham, and Otis Chandler. Well, I said it was a dream, didn't I?

In my youth, had I been told that wistful dreams of conservatism would someday bring me contentment, I surely would have dismissed the matter with a laugh. Liberalism was the banner that I marched under so proudly all those years ago. As this might suggest that I have undergone some sort of political metamorphosis, let me hasten to point out that while the labels have indeed changed, my principles haven't. In my day, a liberal was one who stood for the rights of the individual against the encroachments of the state. The appropriation of the term to one who advocates a monolithic form of government was just one of the many jokers dealt out during FDR's New Deal.

One of the great liberals that I championed, and still regard as one of my great heroes, was the Demos' 1928 presidential candidate, Al Smith. His favorite slogan was "Let's look at the record." If one were to look at the record as interpreted by some of our well-known liberal historians of today, one would find that America was, until 1932, a land of poverty and oppression, as backward as Russia under the Tsars. But in that fateful year, the Saint of Hyde Park rode through Middlesex to warn the embattled farmers, crossed the Delaware to free the slaves, stormed the Bastille, and forced King John to sign the Social Security Act at Runneymede. As one who was there, I have a bit of a problem accepting all of this at face value, especially when they get around to the part about an immaculate conception, but if the record is carefully scrutinized, it will reveal that my vote was one of those that brought the New Deal to power. I must say that even as I was doing so, I had some grave reservations about the FDR philosophy of something for everyone for nothing. Indeed, as the welfare state moved us swiftly and surely to utopia, I couldn't help but feel that heaven was going to be something of an anti-climax. Still, in all, I must give the man his due for the measure of hope that he brought to the country at that darkest hour of the depression. It was a desperate time which required a desperate response. Had he exercised the decency to retire from office when he should have, I could be a great deal more tolerant toward the legacy of his ill-founded, quick-fix solutions that have burdened the country with a bureaucratic morass ever since.

If you sense a teeth-on-edge editorial coming, your perception is correct. In my salad days, there was no more hallowed an American tradition than that the presidency should be limited to two terms for any man, no matter how wise or noble. The example set down by Washington in refusing a third term had virtually become a common law, accepted by both major parties and lauded by political philosophers here and abroad who saw the menace in the "indispensable man." Call it the conclusion of a strabismic old codger if you will, but from my perspective, that break with the Washington-Jefferson-Jackson tradition was a horrendous insult to our political heritage, and I can truthfully state—strident though it might sound—that as a consequence of that abrogation, my life has never been the same.

During the spring of 1940, I held out hope to the very last that the Democratic party would respect its own traditions enough to choose another candidate to lead them. When the fateful announcement came that they were burning their bridges, I felt compelled to do likewise. For the first time in my life, I registered as a Republican, contributed some $10,000 to the Wendell Willkie campaign, helped Robert Montgomery and George Murphy organize a rally at the Los Angeles Coliseum where over one hundred thousand turned out to hear Willkie speak, and for my *piece de resistance*, wrote his campaign song, "We want Willkie."

I was quite the busy little beaver during that campaign, and for several months I turned down all work assignments in order to devote a good twelve hours every day playing Don Quixote to the FDR windmill. As it turned out, however, and this is the part that's hard to believe, despite my song, the electorate didn't want Willkie. But it was a good fight, and at that time I was proud to have been able to devote so much time and money to it.

A few months later, Willkie was asked to appear before a congressional committee to explain some charges that he had made while out on the hustings. "Oh, that," he dismissed with a shrug, "that was just campaign oratory." It was a rather expensive way to learn one of the cardinal rules of politics—never take a candidate more seriously than he takes himself—but it has served me well ever since.

Having been a great deal less than pleased over the president's decision on the third term, my feelings upon learning of his intention to seek a fourth one were somewhat less than joyous. Suffice it to say that I was not a Roosevelt supporter. I wasn't particularly enthused about Mr. Dewey either, but at least it could be said that his campaign wasn't helping to undermine the public's natural response against the intrusion of Big Government, as FDR did by becoming the perennial candidate.

And that, in a rather protracted nutshell, is the saga of the political odyssey that brought me to my pleasant little backyard garden in 1948—which also happened to be the year that I suddenly found myself unemployable in Hollywood. There was quite a bit of panicking on my part when the reality of the situation hit home, but after a very carefully taken financial inventory, my heartbeats stopped registering on the seismographs at Cal Tech. Between Broadway and Hollywood, I had a pretty good run of it, better, in fact, than most writers could hope for. Unfortunately, my ability to invest has never been commensurate with my ability to earn. Translated, this means that I could count my successful transactions on the fingers of one hand and still have enough digits left to play the Minute Waltz. Fortunately, those few that did pay off did so handsomely, so there was no need to take up a collection for the Ryskinds.

At that time, I was fifty-three-years-old. Professionally, I was pleased with the body of work that I had created, and with the financial concerns held in check, it seemed like a sensible point to retire to my garden. As gardens go, it's very pleasant out there. There's a lemon tree and an orange tree and lots of flowers and something always seems to be in bloom. It's not exactly Walden Pond, but it would certainly accommodate my new resolve, which was to spend my remaining days avoiding the madding crowds' ignoble strife. Henceforth, I vowed, my interests would not follow any disputatious avenues, but would reflect the serenity of a sage and slippered philosopher who knew that life was something more than box office grosses and electoral votes (and who was getting tired, frankly, of fighting City Hall and having his brains kicked out in the process).

In preparation for this new lifestyle, I decided to reread Cicero's *De Senectude*, which dealt, I vaguely recalled, with the tranquil delights to be found in a peaceful old age. As luck would have it, my library didn't have a copy of the famous dialogue. Neither did the bookstore I phoned.

"Who published it?" asked the clerk.

"I don't know—probably some firm in Rome," I replied.

"Is it a new book?" he asked.

"Hardly," I replied. "This fellow died in 43 B.C."

He whistled. "We've only been here since 1929. What's it about anyway?" I gave him a synopsis, and he tried to sell me *Life Begins at 40*.

That was discouraging, so I went through my bookshelves again. This time I did come up with Cicero—but it was a volume of his orations against Cataline. Although my Latin was pretty rusty by then, I soon realized that they were disputatious as all get out. This was not what I was looking for, nor was *War and Peace*, whose presence taunted me from the same shelf. I had placed it there many years earlier with a vow to return to it when I was free of the time constraints imposed on a wage earner. With a heaviness of heart which brought back memories of my wife's first attempts at making matzohs, I realized that that day had arrived.

As a person who considered himself well-read, *War and Peace* is a lingering embarrassment. I've taken that bugger on five different times in my life, but I've never been able to get through it. There it is. I've said it, and I'm glad. If this makes me a cultural Philistine, then make the most of it. I know that it's considered to be the world's greatest novel and that no one is really well-rounded until he has mastered this "dictionary of human experience," but will someone please tell me how in the name of Tolstoy are you supposed to keep all the characters straight? Counts, princes, noblemen, dowagers, generals, emperors, and tsars bearing such names as Bezukov, Bolonsky, Bolonskaya, Rostov, Rostova, Kuragin, Kuragina, Karagin, Karagina, Drubetsky, Drubetskaya, Akhrosimova, Hendrikhovna, Dolokov, Kutuzov, Bagratiov, Rostopchin, Mikhailovna, and so on—about five hundred so-ons scattered over 1,600 pages! The brain (at least mine, that is) can't take all of this in, even with a scorecard, which I have used. I can usually stay with it up to the Battle of Austerlitz, but after that, I start getting all of the characters mixed up.

When the movie version came out in the fifties, the Mrs. and I trundled off to the local bijou in hopes of finally filling this great cultural void in our lives. We saw a terrific show, at least until the movie began and we shifted our attention from the teen-age bacchantes directly in front of us to the epic unfolding on the screen. I gave it my undivided attention, believe me I did, but by the time Austerlitz rolled around, damned if I didn't start getting Henry Fonda mixed up with Mel Ferrer. At that point, I threw down my Good 'n' Plenty, grabbed the Mrs. and beat a hasty, uncultured retreat up the aisle. I understand that there is a comic book version of it out now, but I haven't the guts to buy it. To be beaten at that level, which I undoubtedly would be, is the sort of ego damaging risk that I'm not willing to take.

When I made my final go at *W&P* during that spring in which I found myself a man of leisure, I actually made it all the way to the Battle of Smolensk. That's where Napoleon threw in the towel, and, alas, I'm afraid that I did too. With six hundred pages still to go, retirement began to seem less and less attractive. Fortunately, at that time politics became more and more interesting.

Of all the things that could be said about Franklin Roosevelt, the one fact that looms larger perhaps than any other was his impact on the Democratic party. Prior to 1932 it was the party of Jefferson and Jackson; since then, no matter what the label, the Democratic party has been—and I venture to say, will remain for quite some time—an instrument for the perpetuation of the New Deal. This became pretty clear when Harry Truman ran for his own term. What was surprising about that election was the discovery of the inroads the New Deal had made into the Republican party. For all intents and purposes, the platforms of the two parties that year were virtually the same. With the public being offered generic politics, the election pretty much came down to a matter of personalities, and that accounted for the lead that Mr. Dewey maintained until he let it slip through his fingers.

What made the 1948 election memorable for me was the candidacy of Senator Robert A. Taft. Having fought so valiantly, and oftentimes alone, to keep the conservative principles alive throughout the Democratic years, "Mr. Republican" was then, and will forever remain, supreme on my political honor roll.

What I admired the most about Bob Taft was his reverence for the constitution. To him it was gospel, and it was not subject to interpretation. As John F. Kennedy so astutely noted in his *Profiles in Courage*, this was to be Taft's greatness and his tragedy. For he was never the least hesitant about taking unpopular stands on behalf of the precepts he felt to be inviolable; two of which, his criticism of the Nuremberg War trials in 1946 and his co-sponsorship of the Taft-Hartley Labor Act in 1947, were to play a significant part in denying him his justly deserved political rewards.

Having lost six million of my co-religionists to the Nazi genocide, I must admit that my initial reaction to Taft's denouncement of the war trials was not favorable. Coming as it did less than a week before Goering, et al, were to be executed made it seem as if he were speaking in their defense. This, as I was later privileged to learn first hand, was very much the opposite of his intention. He was as thoroughly repulsed by the Nazis as I was, and he was fully aware that his remark, "Vengeance is not justice," would be misconstrued and used against him, but his conscience compelled him to criticize the Nuremberg proceedings for violating the constitution's precepts against *ex post facto* laws. Today, the consensus of opinion seemed to be that Taft's position was correct. For that matter, a good friend, and until his recent passing a neighbor of mine, was Major General Leon Watson. He was the governor of the military conclave at Nuremburg, and even he agreed that America lost more than was gained by the outcome of the trials. But that sentiment was to be of little help to Taft in 1948.

From what I have observed, it would seem that the passage of time has done little to assuage the upper echelons of organized labor who still speak contemptuously of the labor bill that Taft co-sponsored. Nevertheless, Taft was determined to halt the inequities that were being perpetrated under the auspices of the Wagner Act, and again, it was characteristic of him that he had no qualms about introducing legislation that was certain to ignite union reprisals in his native Ohio, one of the most industrialized states in the union. Labor swore to run Taft from office, and it was not an idle threat.

I thought, as did most conservatives with whom I had occasion to speak at that time, that the combination of emotions and events that were working against Taft would prevent him from seeking the '48 nomination. To a lesser man they undoubtedly would have, but Taft was as undaunted in his optimism as he was uncompromising in his integrity. Moreover, he was determined that the liberals would not take permanent possession of the Republican party, and for his efforts to prevent this we can all be grateful.

The news that Taft would run fell on me like sweet lagniappe. I'll admit that I was skeptical about the outcome, but I was thrilled just the same. I placed a bookmark on page 984 of *War and Peace* (It's still there.) and ran about the garden shrieking "Hallelujah!" Beverly Hills, however, takes a dim view of shrieking, especially from a Republican. The neighbors, tolerant folk that they are, will allow an isolated Republican or two, though it means that the intellectual status of the community will probably suffer; a shrieking Republican will definitely result in lower property values—and this, above all, will never be pardoned.

Stifling my euphoria lest the neighbors summon the gendarmes, I ran to my study and dashed off a letter of support to Taft. He responded with a handsome letter welcoming me to the fold, and I felt as if the Fourth of July had come early that year.

There wasn't much that I could do in that campaign other than offer some sorely needed humorous addenda to Taft's standard speech. It didn't help very much, but considering the circumstances, nothing else would have, either. For Taft, despite the brilliance of his political analysis and his winning record, was not a particularly effective campaigner. As an orator he was competent but not distinguished, and as for his general appearance, well, just let it be said that he was never destined to be a media darling.

With the exception of deeply felt political principles, and the courage to stand on them regardless of the consequences, Tom Dewey had everything that Taft didn't. His looks, his speaking voice, and his easy access to wealthy contributors were all to be envied. He also had a campaign organization—largely intact from his previous outing—that was the epitome of the smoothly run, bigtime political machine. Taft didn't stand a chance against it, nor, for that matter, did Truman. That superbly structured machine failed when it was most needed, but as with most mechanical breakdowns, it had more to do with the operator's carelessness than anything else.

After Dewey had thrown the final cog in his own wheel, it was widely acknowledged that the next GOP nomination would go to Taft, who (it's funny how these perceptions can change in retrospect) was then being widely acknowledged as the man who should have been the party's nominee in '48. The one obstacle that Taft had to clear was his senate re-election in '50, and as promised, Labor backed his opponent with a war chest of staggering proportions.

Taft won his re-election bid by his biggest margin ever, but that was in Ohio where his family name had been honored for over one hundred years. Carrying a majority of the other forty-seven states would require a well-organized, precision-operating machine of his own—the very thing that Taft had always disclaimed.

Not long after Taft's re-election, I had the pleasure of meeting a young man who was to play a major role—not only in organizing the Taft For President campaign of '52, but in the conservative movement ever since. This memorable meeting took place when he was presented as the guest lecturer at the Beverly Hills Republican Club. He was on tour promoting his first book, and he was going over in a big way. I was as impressed as everyone else by this young fellow's wit and intelligence, but I remember being somewhat taken aback by his appearance. There was a gauntness about him that was accentuated by his shiny suit and scruffy shoes. I thought back some disturbing memories from the early days of my career as a writer when I was missing as many meals as I was taking. My wife, whose maternal instincts had gone on red alert over the poor fellow's destitution, agreed that something should be done to help him. While our housekeeper was being phoned to prepare a meal, I introduced myself and invited the penniless young author to come home with us. The invitation was accepted, and this was the beginning (borrowing from Humphrey Bogart here) of a "beautiful friendship."

It would be quite an understatement to say that the Ryskind household was captivated by the young man who sat at our kitchen table until the wee hours that night. His charm and intelligence were matched only by his vocabulary—and his commitment to reversing the minority status of conservatism. By the way, the meal that he wolfed down was his second of the evening. This was unknown to me then, as was the fact that he was heir to a family fortune. That was revealed to me two days later at Hollywood Park when I was standing in line to forfeit my first two-dollar bet of the day. I was nearly at the window when I heard my name being called. Looking down the concourse to the line at the $50 window, I saw—still wearing the same shiny suit and scruffy shoes—my new young friend William F. Buckley Jr.

Shortly after achieving his success with *God and Man at Yale,* Bill and I found ourselves working together for the first time. This happened in New York when I returned for the *Of Thee I Sing* revival. Forrest Davis asked me to join a delegation which included Bill, John Chamberlain and Ralph de Toledano. Our purpose was to call on General Albert Wedemeyer, who had been the commander of the American forces in China, Burma, and India during the war. The general had been asked but was uncertain about accepting the chairmanship of the Taft campaign. Having retired from the army, the general was then serving on the board of directors at Avco Industries. Since Avco was receiving government contracts, accepting a position with a political campaign would mean that he would have to take an extended leave of absence, if not resign his position altogether, in order to avoid a conflict of interest. In either case, he would be subjecting himself to considerable financial loss—hence the hesitation—and in light of my own experience in this area, I can't say that I blamed him in the least. As it turned out though, it took very little persuasion on our part to get a commitment from the general. The state department's postwar record of appeasement with the Communists in China (the general had very close ties to Chiang Kai-shek during the war), the Korean War stalemate, then entering the second year, and especially President Truman's dismissal of Douglas MacArthur, the general's former commander, had already done our job for us.

One of General Wedemeyer's first functions in his new capacity as National Chairman of the Taft For President Committee was to ask John Dos Passos and myself to co-chair the campaign's Arts and Letters Committee. It was an honor that both of us readily accepted, but our positions were, regretfully, to be more honorary than practical. I'm afraid that this was one of the biggest mistakes in a campaign that was to produce an inordinate amount of them. Celebrity endorsements have always been an integral part of political campaigns, and in 1952, the year television was to completely change the entire political spectrum, their necessity took on an importance that was all too self-evident. We had a large roster of Taft supporters in Hollywood on which we could have drawn, but Taft was disdainful of the traditional hoopla of politics. He wanted only to run on his commendable record. This was commendable in itself, but hardly a practical stance to be taken in the face of the heavy artillery that was being wheeled in his path.

The "big gun" of my military metaphor was, of course, General Eisenhower. Because Ike had never voted, it was assumed by those of us who were contributing to the Taft strategy that if the general were persuaded to trade in on his enormous (and justified) popularity, his close ties with FDR and Truman would lead him to do so under the banner of the Democrats. This would have been welcomed, as it would have made for an election in which the platforms of the opposing parties would have been more clearly divided than they had been in quite some time.

What was not welcomed were the invidious manipulations of the eastern wing of the Republican party—specifically those of Henry Cabot Lodge Jr.—that brought General Eisenhower into the GOP for the expressed purpose of denying Bob Taft the nomination that he had every moral right to call his own.

As if contending with Ike's enormous popularity weren't enough of a challenge, Taft was also to find himself the target of labor's renewed vendetta. They got their worst licks in during the New Hampshire primary by instructing those in their fold who were registered as Democrats to re-register as Republicans and vote for Eisenhower. This was a big help in giving Ike the state, and with it came the psychological boost of being the front runner.

With the Eisenhower bandwagon rolling at full throttle after New Hampshire, all of the pundits were writing Taft off altogether. I'll have to admit that even I was not optimistic about the outcome of the primaries. Taft, however, was not deterred in the least. He continued campaigning in his stolid, uncompromising manner, and to everyone's surprise, including mine, he very nearly brought it off.

When I arrived at the Taft headquarters in Chicago a week before the convention convened, the figures that were being bounced around by the press had Ike winning by a lopsided margin on the first ballot. The sheaf of telegrams from Taft supporters that General Wedemeyer showed me indicated otherwise. The tally of those pledges had Taft less than one hundred votes shy of the nomination. With several hundred delegates still uncommitted, it was anything but a closed race.

The central issue in the bitter fight that followed lay with which side would be awarded the sixty-eight delegates from Texas. Ike had won them by actual count in the primary, but as so many of them were re-registered Democrats, the convention was to rule whether or not they would be seated. It was a valid point of dispute, which was resolved, tragically, by some of the dirtiest politics on record.

A great deal of the dirty work that transpired in Chicago could be attributed to that Pillar of Pity, Henry Cabot Lodge Jr. I had my first exposure to it when I checked into the Hilton. There was a large banner strung across the lobby which suggested, none too cleverly, that Robert A. Taft's initials could be acronymed into RAT. Other banners in other hotels were even less subtle: THOU SHALT NOT STEAL being the most odious of that most sorry lot. I was infuriated to the verge of nausea that Lodge would attempt to taint the name of as honorable a man as ever drew a breath. It's been said that one of the marks of a gentleman is that he says only the good things of the dead. In the case of Mr. Lodge, I find, even to this day, it takes a very, very large effort for me to honor that requisite.

Lodge was by no means alone in his determination to railroad Taft out of the nomination. There were many instances in several of the delegations of men being told that bank loans that they had made might be suddenly called unless they voted the right way. But that was small time in comparison to the patronage coercion used by that master arm-twister Tom Dewey. As always, New York was to play a crucial role in the election process, and Dewey ruled that state's delegation with an iron hand. On the eve of the convention he called a meeting of his delegates and told them frankly: "I understand that some of you intend to vote to seat the Taft group from Texas. You can do that, of course, but I'm still the governor of New York, and if you do, I promise you'll be dropped from any state post. And what's more, I'll see to it that you never hold such a post again."

I was in General Wedemeyer's office that night when some of those we had counted on came in to tell him their story. They were mostly young men who were shouldering the financial burdens of starting families. They hated Dewey, of course, but they hated themselves even more as they explained what they were going to do—and why. The general nodded his understanding, and they slunk out. When they had left, he turned to me, his voice breaking, and said, "God! Is this what America is coming to?"

I sat with the general in his box seat and watched the defection as the pro-Ike measure carried, and with it the nomination. It was a crushing loss, but of all of us that were in the Taft headquarters that night, the one who bore up under it the best was Senator Taft himself. There would be other fights, he assured us, but it would be Taft's spirit and not the Senator who would lead his followers in them. Less than a year after that terrible night in Chicago, the Father of Modern Conservatism was taken from us, and as with every other aspect of his life, that sudden ordeal with cancer was marked by his unflinching courage.

It was a testament to the greatness of Robert Alphonso Taft that, in conjunction with his eulogies, political analysts also began eulogizing the entire conservative movement. The unpleasant truth of the matter was that it was pretty hard to disagree with their assertion. Taft simply had been conservatism in America for the preceding fifteen years, and at that time, there just wasn't anybody to take his place.

Certainly one of the most instrumental factors in the final triumph of conservatism in this country was *National Review*. I can't say how long Bill Buckley had dreamed of presenting the conservative philosophy in a magazine format, but I do remember listening to a very detailed account of his hopes for making it become a reality shortly after we met. After the thunderclap of Bob Taft's death left us all numbly staring into an enormous void, Bill called to ask for my assistance in putting his plan to work. It was the right move at the right time, and I was anxious to help in any way that I could.

Money, of course, was the first concern. The only experience that I had in the specialized art of fund-raising was through "backers' auditions" in New York. This is the process that producers use to get their shows mounted on Broadway. A group of angels (people with some loose cash) will be invited to an apartment, the playwright will outline the story board, the composer will jump in and play the musical numbers at the appropriate time, and pledges will be solicited when it's over. It's a system that has served Broadway well since its beginnings, and I saw no reason why it shouldn't serve our purpose as well.

Bob Arthur, a good friend and neighbor of mine, who was then producing movies for Francis-the-Talking Mule, and Cary-the-Talking Grant, was kind enough to help me get everything organized. We set up a series of receptions here at the house, Bob would pour everyone a drink, Bill would explain what he hoped to do with the magazine, and I would ask everyone to write a $1,000 pledge. I must say, it turned out better than we had hoped. All in all, we must have raised about half the money that launched *National Review* in this manner. I should also like to mention that special thanks are due Patrick Frawley and Henri Salvatori—both of whom were to later become charter members of the Reagan "kitchen cabinet"—for their generosity when those checks were being written.

I hadn't planned on any further involvement with *National Review* after our fund-raising sessions, but Bill, who is no slouch in the persuasion department, asked me to accept a membership on the board of directors and to serve as a long-distance contributing editor. I wasn't quite sure just what I was letting myself in for (any title with the word "director" in it still makes me uneasy), but I said that I would give it my best effort.

It took the best efforts of quite a few very dedicated people—far too many to mention here, regretfully—but through their tireless efforts, the first issue of *National Review* hit the stands on 19 November 1955 with, I'm pleased to remember, a cover article by yours truly.

Having expended as much time and energy as I did to *National Review's* debut, I was quite touched when a package from Bill arrived a few days before Christmas that year. It was placed under our Christmas tree, and on the holiday morning I had the pleasure of finding that my new editor-in-chief was so taken with my contribution that he sent me 1,200 *NR* pamphlets with a note to please distribute them wherever I could.

Scroogeisms aside, one couldn't have asked to work for a better editor. The only stipulation that Bill made concerning my submissions was that they should be "the D——est piece of prose published in 2,000 years this side of Mesopotamia." (Herbert Bayard Swope lives!)

In many ways, *National Review* in its early years reminded me of the old days with Swope at the *World*. Certainly in the grand manner and high standards of the respective editors, and most certainly in the writers who flocked to their fold to share in that patina. For not only was *NR* to become home to such former radicals turned conservatives as Max Eastman, John Dos Passos, and myself, but in the Swope tradition, it was also to nurture and launch a new crop of noted political writers such as Brent Bozell and Joan Didion—yes, the Joan Didion of the fictional angst fame—and a young pup whose surname just happens to be the same as mine.

Career-wise I am also grateful to *National Review*, for it was on the basis of my work there that Nick Williams, a fine gentleman and then editor of the *Los Angeles Times*, asked me to begin my column. In retrospect, it might not have been the wisest of moves for a sixty-five-year-old man with a history of ulcers to trade in the leisurely responsibility of delivering an essay once a month for the Sisyphean pressures of a twice-weekly column, but at the time, it seemed a wonderful opportunity had arrived. California, especially southern California, had become one of the most important constituencies in the country thanks to the postwar boom. As California goes, so goes the nation, and I was determined to see a conservative take the White House in my lifetime.

Having been at this pundit business some twenty-five years now, I have turned out over two thousand of these alluring, erudite, suitable-for-framing columns of flawless logic and deathless prose. For my efforts, I have received something in excess of two hundred thousand letters (Would that my stock investments had that kind of return.). This was an occupational hazard for which I was ill-prepared. Because it is an undeniable fact that every commentator, whatever his political philosophy, learns from his mail that his readers fall into two distinct categories: there are the rational, civilized, literate, and far-seeing folk who agree with him: and there are the benighted, uncultured, primitively extremist, and fantastically bigoted barbarians who disagree.

The first group, of course, presents no problem; the members thereof are perfectly capable of taking care of themselves and rendering the right literary and economic decisions. It is always a pleasure to hear from them.

Unfortunately, in my own case the records disclose that these high-minded citizens are outnumbered by the second group, malcontents who—to judge by their voluminous missives—are obviously going through a vast population explosion and offer living testimony of the dangers predicted by Malthus. They don't produce enough cerebral food to nourish their brain cells even now, and goodness knows what their mental processes will be when they have to stretch that little among even more people.

These are the kooks who offer dubious data and warn of horrendous cabals. They see a Jewish conspiracy to rule the world, can show by the Bible that Negroes are not human beings, and assert that the Vatican is tunneling a secret passage to the White House. All of which is supported by forged documents, citations from other kooks, and the tortuous sort of cryptology by which it is proved that either Bacon or Roger Manners, the fifteenth Earl of Rutland, the seventeenth Earl of Oxford, or the nineteenth Earl of Scheib really wrote the plays attributed to Shakespeare.

For the first few weeks after I opened for business, I was so flattered that anyone was actually paying attention to what I had to say, that I actually managed to answer each of the fifty-sixty letters that I received each day. But, alas, mine is a one-man operation, run by a factotum who is chief cook and bottle washer and only a two-fingered typist. Thus the courtesy was understandably (at least it was to me) discontinued, though every letter was carefully read. Naturally, this was interpreted as a snub, which only served to egg most of my correspondents into writing yet another letter in which arrogance was added to their original charges that I was either a crypto-Fascist or a crypto-Communist. But so far, no one has ever accused me of being a crypto-neutral, and that, at least, is something.

There are a tremendous number of other hazards associated with this business (or racket) of columning—often known as calumny—not the least of which is the actual writing of the piece. This in itself was never a problem, but dealing with the time differential was. Today a writer can sit in his study and type into some sort of Buck Rogers gizmo that electronically connects him to his publisher. When I started out on this enterprise in 1960, that luxury wasn't available. My columns had to be

in the *Times* office two days in advance or there wouldn't
be enough time to get them mimeographed and mailed
to the rest of the papers that were carrying me. This
meant that I had to mail it from my home three days in
advance to get it to the *Times* before their syndication
deadline. This tended to have a somewhat ill effect on my
attempts at writing about up-to-the-minute issues. And
although I am a member of the same tribe that produced
visionaries such as King Solomon and Arthur Schlesinger
Jr., the fates, in direct violation of the Declaration of
Independence, have not distributed their gifts equally.
My portion, then, the story of my life really, was to be two
days behind what was happening. This wasn't bad, I suppose, as there were many readers who were wont to point
out that my writing suggested that two centuries would
be a more appropriate number.

I don't wish to sound cynical about this, but with the
mail system being what it is, I was grateful that my columns made it to the *Times* on time as many times as they
did. Many—far more than I care to remember—was the
time on deadline morning when Nick Williams' secretary
would call with word that my piece hadn't arrived in the
early mail. That would be the standby signal for the Mrs.
to back the Wreck of the Hesperus out of the garage.
After the late morning mail came in, I would get another
call from the *Times*. If the column was still missing, then
the wife (since I can't operate a toaster, let alone an
automobile) would have to hand-carry the original copy
to Williams' office. Thankfully, the postal service would
come through about 99 percent of the time—and I would
hear the jubilant huzzahs in the background while getting
the good news over the phone. (They really love literature at the *Times*.)

The New Frontier: the Promised Land, as foreseen by
the prophets of Harvard, was the subject of most of the
early editorials. I had hoped during the campaign, that
the New Frontier wouldn't be a warmed-up version of the
New Deal. That hope died during Mr. Kennedy's inaugu-

ral speech when he got to the part about "never negotiating from fear, but never fearing to negotiate." A less
intrepid man might have decided after Yalta, Teheran
and Potsdam that, when it comes to Russia, "All we have
to fear" is "negotiations," but that wouldn't have fit with
Camelot's credo as exemplified at the Bay of Pigs and the
Berlin Wall of "talk big, but keep your powder wet."

Although I took exception with almost every decision
made by Mr. Kennedy during his brief stay in office, I am
not one to withhold credit where credit is due. In that
vein, I would like to state my regard for the young
president's handling of the missile crisis in Cuba. It was
a frightening situation, and we can remain grateful for
Mr. Kennedy's judicious use of America's restraint and
resolve.

In looking back over the relentless succession of anguish that occurred between that fateful day in Dallas and
Richard Nixon's resignation ten-and-a-half years later, the
image that comes to mind is one of America caught up
in some sort of Rod Serling time warp in which
Shakespeare had thrust Hamlet, Claudius and Laertes,
Caesar, Brutus and Marc Antony, Othello and Iago, Richard the Third, King Lear, Macbeth, and Coriolanus center stage in a tragedy that would never end. That we did
survive as a nation was no small miracle, and for that, I
continued to give thanks for the miraculousness of our
constitution.

Vietnam was, of course, the central issue of that decade of strife. While I'm sure that no one suffered more
than Lyndon Johnson over the dissension that nearly
toppled us as a result of our involvement there, the unpleasant truth of the matter remains that most of the
discord was the result of his deceitful campaign posture
in 1964. If the president, who made such political hay out
of tagging Barry Goldwater as a warmonger, had the
integrity to inform the electorate that his post-election
plans for an escalation in Vietnam were virtually the same
as Barry's, there would not have been that staggering

mandate. Without it, there would not have been a Great
Society, and therein lay the trouble. For if the sixties
taught us nothing else, let it be remembered that no
president can deliver guns and butter at the same time.
And to that I would append, that when our young men
are dying on distant battlefields, it is nothing short of
sacrilege for a president to even make such an attempt.

There were 27 million of us who were hoping that the
history of that time would be written from the far more
honorable perspective that a Goldwater presidency would
have provided. As one of the spokesmen for our group,
I devoted almost an entire year's worth of columns toward the realization of that goal. The results weren't
quite what I had been hoping for, but neither were about
90 percent of the other candidacies that I've supported
over the years.

Again, I'm indebted to the Beverly Hills Republican
Club, for it was there that I first met Barry when he came
out one evening to be our guest speaker. This was in the
early sixties, and at that time, Barry was also writing a
twice weekly column for the *Los Angeles Times*. We were
alternating days, and on those days when we weren't
carried, the space would be covered by either Bill Buckley,
Ray Moley, John Chamberlain, Ralph de Toledano, and—
for a while—by Richard Nixon. In light of the *Times* of
today, that would seem to be on a probability par with
Lou Grant editing *Human Events*, but it actually was true
back then.

By that time, Barry had firmly established himself as
the rightful inheritor of the Taft mantle, and I very much
wanted to meet him. With the *Times* as our mutual link,
we hit it off from the word go (another beautiful friendship), and I was only too happy to have a go at lightening
up several of his speeches over the next couple of years.

I suppose it was inevitable that the new standard-
bearer of conservatism would inherit many of the same
problems that plagued his predecessors. The biggest of
them was having to fend off the incessant flank attacks

being made by the liberal wing of the GOP. For Taft, these came from Dewey, Kuchel, and Henry Cabot Lodge Jr.; for Barry, they came from Romney, Rockefeller, and Henry Cabot Lodge Jr., who was, if nothing else, consistent. It just didn't seem to register with this group that there was a conservative wing to the party who were tired of being disenfranchised after so many years of hard work for the party's good. Considering the debt that was owed to us, a turnabout of fair play would have seemed in order when Barry won the nomination fair and square. But I'm sure glad that I didn't hold my breath while waiting for it to happen.

I'm moved to that astringency mainly from my memories of Nelson Rockefeller. Unquestionably, there was much greatness in the man. Although born to the purple, he never fell for the lures of cafe society, but instead, dedicated his life to public service. He chaired important delegations commissioned by FDR, Truman, and Eisenhower, and twice presided over the government of New York State. Despite his record of achievements, or perhaps because of it, Rocky always seemed to come across as abrasively condescending. The phrase that leaps to mind—from some forgotten volume—is "the unconscious insolence of conscious opulence." If the game couldn't be played according to his rules, it wouldn't be played at all.

The first of Rocky's attempts at being the GOP's quadrennial spoiler happened in 1960. When an exploratory cross-country tour told him that Nixon was the party's overwhelming favorite, he promptly began proclaiming that he didn't know where Nixon stood. Although Nixon's record as a congressman, senator, and vice-president was written in rather large print, Rocky would have none of it. Almost every night one could catch him on the TV panels with that one ringing question: "Where does Nixon stand?" It didn't interfere with Nixon's rounding up of delegates, but it kept Rockefeller trim, sprinting from one station to another. And the

Democrats loved his act and began imitating it with the greatest of success.

Finally, on the eve of his convention, Nixon met with Rockefeller one midnight for what became known as the Treaty of Fifth Avenue. Rockefeller said what he wanted in the party platform, and Nixon, thinking of New York's forty-five electoral votes, agreed. This caused quite a ruckus at the convention, and there undoubtedly would have been a conservative walkout had Barry not quelled the mutiny (justified in his opinion) with a plea for party unity.

As it turned out, 1960 was only Rocky's warm-up act. From Rocky himself—and from all headquarters—there came almost paranoic blasts of hate against Barry throughout the '64 primaries. And, of course, afterward too. The Arizonan was pictured as a combination of the worst features of Caligula, Nero, Rasputin, the Black Plague, and Dr. Strangelove. He—and the rest of his followers, too—was not only antediluvian, but anti-Semitic (top that, if you can).

It was here in California that the Rockefeller anti-Goldwater virulence was at its worst. I had breakfast one morning with Barry not long before that crucial primary, when it happened that the *Los Angeles Times* carried another front page Rockefeller blast at him. "Don't you think that you ought to fire at least one back?" I asked.

He grinned as though the notion was not too disdainful. But he shook his head. "I feel I owe the party too much to do anything divisive, and so I'm aiming only at the Democrats. Of course, I resent this dirty pool, but I'm damned if I'll play it."

Well, Barry won that primary, which gave him the nomination without having to play dirty pool. Nor did those of us who were backing him ever have to play Nelson's game either. To this day, many people—and many of those people know the truth of the matter—still maintain that Rockefeller was booed by the Goldwater delegates when he rose to speak at the convention. I sat

in with the California delegates that night, and saw no
delegate join in the cat calls. That came entirely from the
gallery, solid for Barry and understandably bitter at a
man whose organization had denounced Goldwater ad-
herents as the scum of American society. Maybe they
shouldn't have booed—but on the other hand, Rocky's
own phrases had not been the sort to win friends or
influence people—except, maybe, to boo.

Aside from the internecine warfare of the GOP and
the lopsided voter tally that it helped to produce, what
made that election such an especially bitter pill for me to
swallow was observing the violence committed by the
press against their number one priority—objectivity. I'm
speaking here primarily of the print media, because television—as God and His counselors at CBS News will attest
—has been an electronic conduit of the liberal establishment since its inception.

As a cub reporter under Herbert Bayard Swope's
tutelage, I was taught to stick to the four Ws—Who, What,
Where, and When. Through slanted phrases and the subtle
innuendo of the qualifying objective, reporters can always editorialize by the inclusion of the fifth W—Why, but
to do so is to break with the journalistic equivalent of the
Hippocratic Oath. In 1964, the evidence of that oath
being disregarded became alarmingly ubiquitous, even—
I'm sorry to state—in the once-staid reportage of the *Los
Angeles Times* where the proportions often seemed to
become those of a stiff martini: five to one, and you could
hardly notice the vermouth of facts at all.

Throughout that election year and most of the following years as well, I felt compelled to take issue with the
Times over the incidences of interpretative reporting that
appeared under its masthead. The *Times* responded by
censoring those references in my columns—sentences at
first, then paragraphs, and then double paragraphs. This
seemed to run contrary to their stated policy "... that the
opinionated columnists who were writing for the 'Times'
ought to speak out on these editorial pages, whether or

not their ideas were generally popular, or whether the 'Times' agreed with them. For if the 'Times,' or any other newspaper or magazine or television network excluded those with whom it disagreed, that indeed would be the betrayal of a free exchange of ideas."

Noble sentiments indeed. With that thought in mind, you might imagine my thoughts on that morning (October 30, 1965), when an associate editor of the *Times* called in to inform me that Nick Williams refused to run the column that I had just submitted. He was the employer, and I was the employee. This was his undeniable right, though I questioned his judgment. You know writers.

About a half hour later I received a call from the *Times* syndication office informing me that the *Times* would not release the column to the 37 other papers that ran my work, and would I please write a column about something else—anything else—instead. This, I refused to do, because it assumed that the editorial policy of the *Times* was *ipso facto* the judgment of the other papers. I thought that the editors of the various papers who ran my column were all of legal age and should be allowed to decide for themselves whether the column was printable. Otherwise, I would regard my contract with the syndicate at an end. I stood pat, the *Times* stood pat, and that was that.

In response to a query from *Editor and Publisher* magazine, the *Times* expressed their standpoint. "The column was an unjustified attack on the press in general and the Associated Press in particular," said Rex Barley, manager of the Los Angeles Times Syndicate. "There was absolutely no objection to the viewpoint expressed, but it was pegged on incorrect facts."

Mr. Barley's charge of inaccuracy boiled down to one word, "anonymous." Not that this is a Federal case or anything, but for the record, here's the paragraph that stirred up the whole fuss.

"And I still think Melville Stone is turning over in his

resting place at what has happened to the AP since his day—the Stone Age. A recent AP dispatch told of the Kennedy's withdrawing of the name of a family friend for a Federal judgeship. And at the end followed the anonymous reporter's speculations as to why—which took as much space as the story. The inside story or a reporter's guess—who knows? But it all came under the heading of bona fide news."

In the E&P article, Mr. Barley went on to explain that the AP dispatch came with a byline, thus voiding my assertion of anonymity. That may well have been the case, but when I read the story, of all places on the front page of the *L.A. Times,* it ran without a byline. And if that's not anonymous, what is?

I think it pertinent to mention here, that the *Times* extended an editorial olive branch to me. I spent about two months mulling it over, but decided, with the utmost regret, that I couldn't accept it. A large part of my decision about not returning to the *Times* was based on the fact that when the *Times* rejected the offending column, I had copies of it made and sent to the first fifteen papers on my list of subscribers with a note attached, asking if the column had come through the regular channels, would its subject matter have prevented it from being run. Well, all of those papers did run it, and some of them accompanied it with an editorial attacking the *Times* for trying to do their thinking for them—and that included several papers whose political philosophy ran contrary to mine.

But the biggest reason that I felt that I could no longer continue with the *Times* was the fact that the *Times* had become a newspaper whose political philosophy ran contrary to mine. To anyone with an appreciation of the *L.A. Times's* legacy, its editorial about-face during the early years of the 60s bordered on the supernatural. Because for the better part of this century, together with two other strategically located big-city papers, the *New York Daily News* and the *Chicago Tribune*, it had formed the Big Three which had kept the banner of traditional conservatism flying from East to West without dipping its colors from the New Deal to the New Frontier.

To remind myself that this once was true, I still have a commemorative editorial signed by Otis Chandler III (scion of the founding family) on the occasion of the *Times* eightieth anniversary: "Our editorial policy will remain unchanged. We are a conservative Republican newspaper dedicated to the protection and preservation of individual freedoms under God and as guaranteed under our Constitution." Three years after that statement appeared, the Western fortress of the Old Guard Triumvirate was backing Rockefeller in the California primary.

In the years since my departure from the *Times*, it has firmly established itself with the *New York Times* and the *Washington Post* at the forefront of Liberalism in America, although that point seems lost on young Chandler who has recently gone on record to counter the charges of the *Times* liberal bias by stating that it was neither leftist nor rightist, but a "centrist" paper. If he was referring to the ideological centerground shared by Jane Fonda and the British Labor Party, I would agree with that assessment. If he was referring to the traditional political spectrum, I'm afraid that the *Times* has missed that center mark by about 180 degrees.

If Mr. Chandler really can't detect the liberal bias of his publication, I strongly suspect that he's been skipping over its op-ed page for the past couple of decades—a practice which I wish I had the sense to do. One of the traditional hallmarks of a newspaper's political outlook has always been its editorial cartoon. And if Paul Conrad is a centrist, I'm the Queen of Romania (borrowing from Dottie Parker here).

Conrad is widely syndicated and is regarded in Establishment circles as a great wit. But not by me. His humor is too often colored by sheer malice rather than wit. True, three or four times a year, he comes across with a lalapalooza that tickles my funny bone, but that gives him a batting average of about .050, which is hardly Big League.

Of late, he has harped on one pun (if that's what it is), which consists of incessantly portraying the President as "Reagan Hood," who steals from the poor to give to the rich. Puns on names are too easy to be used constantly. Thus, I might refer to the cartoonist as Paul Comrade—a favorite term for "pal" in the Communist argot—as a buzzword to indicate his near-Marxism outlook. But I'd certainly not use it 95 times in 100 columns.

By far, though, the worst of Conrad's efforts come when he displays his total ignorance about the laws of versification: His meter stumbles, and it is clear, he doesn't know his rhyme from his assonance.

Although our tenures at the *Times* overlapped by a year, I've never met Conrad. Mutual friends tell me that he speaks contemptuously of me, and I must say, with some gratification, that I would be very displeased with myself were that not the case. So there.

And there I was, 70-years-old and unemployed once again because of politics. I took some comfort in the fact that for the first time in my life, the decision was mine, although the distinction became somewhat blurry the first time that the monthly check didn't arrive. Just what my future would be, I didn't know, and at that time, I didn't particularly care. The holiday season was approaching, and for the first time in many years, all of the family made it home, bringing a few new additions in tow. The double bonus of reunion plus being able to wake up to an unscheduled day seemed a luxury of the highest order. After a fortnight of it, I was giving some pretty serious thought to letting things remain that way.

It happened during this time that I was honored by the Beverly Hills Republican Club for my twenty-five years of membership. It was an event that I had mixed feelings about, as some sort of thank-you speech would be required and I had long since retired—undefeated—as the world's worst speaker with a self-promise to rest on my laurels thereafter. Although it had been some time since I last tested my form, my remarks that evening proved conclusively that I was still the undisputed title holder.

Aside from my jitters, that evening was truly an affair to remember—eight hundred people dressed to the nines, ponying up a hefty per-plate tribute (proceeds to charity) for a dinner at the Beverly Hilton. Mayor Yorty sent a Certificate of Meritorious Service, George Murphy made some flattering remarks, as did Gaylord Parkinson, Chairman of the State Republican Committee, and John Wayne, Buddy Ebsen and Raymond Massey put on a skit afterwards. The lot of a columnist may be a lonely one, but when the rewards come, they seem to more than make up for it.

I mention all of this, because it was that dinner which ended the retirement that I was enjoying so much. Bill Buckley, who had flown out to be the guest speaker of the evening, concluded his talk with an appeal for me to get back in the harness. This brought an ovation which rattled me as few things had before. In the parlance of "The Godfather," it was "an offer that I couldn't refuse," and to be honest about it, deep down I really didn't want to anyway.

I was grateful to Bill Buckley for making the arrangements for me with the Washington Star syndicate, which was also distributing his columns. I regained most of the papers that had been carrying me, and those that were lost were replaced by new subscribers. In Los Angeles, I had exchanged the *Times*, which had a substantial circulation lead over the *Examiner*, but the loss was offset by my acquisition of several of the smaller papers in the surrounding area, so I pretty much broke even over the deal.

At any rate, I was presented to a sizeable readership, and there was much to be done. The Establishment's funereal orations on the demise of conservatism were being pronounced on an almost daily basis after Barry went down to defeat. While there was no denying that it was a stinging loss, there were a great many of us who regarded the fact that a conservative had finally been able to capture the nomination as a victory. The task that lay ahead was to maintain the momentum without losing what had been gained. Interesting challenge.

It was a challenge that was more than met, and a great deal of the credit goes to the American Conservative Union. This was the post-'64 election brainchild of a group led by Rep. John Ashbrook of Ohio, and Kudos to him with a capital K, as it has turned out to be one of the most effective political action groups ever organized. I devoted a great deal of column space towards the ACU's fruition, with some very gratifying results. Unfortunately, many of the contributors made their checks out to me, all of which were immediately (well, as fast as the Mrs. and I could type) returned with instructions for forwarding them to the proper destination. It was a time consuming effort, but many thanks just the same to those who cared enough to get involved.

Having learned my lesson the hard way, I declined an offer to serve on the ACU's board of directors. Any commentator worth his salt must be free to criticize an organization should it not live up to its original intentions. This was never to be the case with ACU, but my membership in the John Birch Society was a different matter.

I first met Robert Welch in the late 50s, after having corresponded with him for several years. I had admired his thoughtful, well-written pieces, especially "The Life of John Birch," which I found to be an intensely moving account of a young American who was killed by the Chinese Communists, and which I would still recommend. As a result, I subscribed to his magazine, "American Opinion," which was running some excellent articles: William Schlamm surveying Europe through some very penetrating eyes, Holmes Alexander's insightful series on the Federalist Papers, and Welch himself making a sharp analysis of the steady growth of Soviet power.

During this time, Welch wrote "The Politician," which was basically an expanded personal letter to a small group of us in the conservative movement. The manuscript contained both unimpeachable facts—the gains communism had made during the Roosevelt, Truman and Eisenhower administrations—with completely impeachable conclusions—that FDR, Truman and Ike were themselves part of the Soviet conspiracy. This was not only dumb, it was dangerous.

I had lunch with Bob when he came to Los Angeles in preparation for the founding of the JBS. When he asked for my opinion of his manuscript, I told him that if it were ever published, he would be doing a frightful damage to a cause which he had the potential to serve so nobly. Apparently this had been the opinion of everyone that he had shown it to. He asked me to give the manuscript back, which I did, at which he promised that it would be filed away. In our further discussion, he promised that *The Politician* would not be the basis of the JBS, and that any member would be free to openly criticize the organization should he feel the need. I had some strong reservations about what I was letting myself in for, but I had a stronger hope that they would be proven wrong by the establishment of a national anti-communist organization which I felt was badly needed.

I'm not the greatest go-to-meetings type, which accounts for the fact that I only made it to three meetings during the two years that I belonged to the JBS. I don't know what happened in other parts of the country, but at the local chapter here in Los Angeles, nobody hailed anybody, nobody saluted any fuhrer, and no plans were laid down to take over the country. At the first meeting, I saw a film, *Operation Abolition*; at the second one, the documentary *Communism on the Map*; and at the third, we were urged to get our friends to wire congress to stand firm on the Connolly Amendment. It all seemed well-organized and worthwhile, and I was glad to be a part of it.

When I began my column with the *Times*, I quietly set about to resign from the various organizations to which I belonged, including the JBS. Unfortunately, this was at

the same time that Welch launched into his Impeach Earl
Warren campaign, which landed me in another one of
those damned if I do, damned if I don't quandaries that
I seem to be forever encountering. I regarded Warren's
tenure on the Supreme Court as one of the most misguided in our judicial history, but he was certainly not
guilty of an impeachable act. It was a silly waste of time
to even consider it, and as I had feared, the repercussions
were swift in coming.

Excerpts from *The Politician* were used by the press in
the ensuing attack on the JBS. I thought that this was
unfair, because at least 90 percent of the members had
never seen that manuscript. To resign at that point would
seem to validate the charge that the entire organization
had taken Welch's personal dogma to heart. When Welch
pulled back on his attack, the furor blew over, and when
things quieted down, I did resign, as did a great many
others who were equally disillusioned at the unsteadiness
of the JBS's founder.

Not long after that, Welch, in his apparent zeal to be
the twentieth century John Brown, was back at it again.
His charges that Ike was a Communist were not made in
a private letter, or to the JBS, but to the press. He was
acting like a damned fool, and I felt obliged to say as
much in an open letter to him in my column. I could
applaud his patriotism, and I could understand much of
his frustration, but frustration not held in check with
common sense will destroy a man, which is exactly what
happened to Robert Welch.

It strikes me as ironic, tragically ironic I suppose, that
Richard Nixon, who was an early and an outspoken critic
of Robert Welch, should also fall victim to a foolish dis-
regard for common sense.

The feeling that I held about Dick Nixon throughout
his active political career was that he was not a true
conservative, but that he would certainly do until the real
thing came along. Accordingly, I supported all of his
campaigns, even (and no Republican has ever been subjected to a greater test of party loyalty) when he ran with

Henry Cabot Lodge Jr. Although I was in open disagreement with some of his activities, there was never a time when I doubted the greatness of the man. I still have no hesitancy about stating that he was, in my opinion, the president with the greatest knowledge of foreign affairs in our history. For the good of the country, let alone partisan politics, this was an ability that should not have been squandered.

My association with Dick Nixon goes back to the '47 HUAC hearings. We were introduced in the hallway of the House Building, but this was nothing more than a handshake and an exchange of amenities before he was called back to his office. The next time we met was here at this house about two years later. Don Jackson, who was our congressman for seven terms, always stopped by to say hello when he was in town. Don had become something of a mentor to Dick, and one day he brought his young protege with him. He was urging Dick to run for the upcoming senate seat, and to this, I concurred wholeheartedly. Dick was uncertain about taking the chance, but I'm happy that he took Don's advice, as he was probably the only person who could have beaten Helen Gahagan Douglas that year. My contribution to the campaign was to assist Dick's speechwriters. I suppose there was a touch of irony to this also, as I had once written a film for Melvyn Douglas, who was married to Miss Gahagan.

After the election, the Nixons honored us by coming to dinner. It was a quiet affair, but very memorable in that the stiff, formal, somewhat awkward public Richard Nixon, who has always been such an easy target for the comedians and the caricaturists, was definitely not the man who came to dinner. With his guard down he was warm, gracious, and very witty. Why he doesn't—or perhaps can't—present this side of his personality to the public, I'll leave to others (and God knows, he must have been the most psychoanalyzed man in history), but I remember him as being one of the most companionable guests that I've ever entertained.

We parted that night in a spirit of high cheer. The next time I saw Dick, it was all I could do to restrain myself from cursing. This took place about a year later, when I was in New York as part of the delegation that called on General Wedemeyer. Ralph de Toledano called me at my hotel one night, just as I was about to go to bed. He said that Dick was in town and wanted to see us. I got dressed and went to Ralph's apartment, where George Sokolsky and a few others had already arrived. Dick showed up a few minutes later and announced that he was sorry, but he would be supporting Ike and not Taft for the nomination. He had held up his finger to the political wind and decided that it would be in his best interests to jump on the "but" bandwagon. "Yes, Taft is the most qualified man for the job, 'but' he can't be elected." If a few prominent Republicans would have stood firm, and Dick Nixon was one of those that we were counting on heavily to do so, that bandwagon could have been stopped.

Despite the bad feelings generated by Dick's decision to align himself with Ike, I couldn't help but admire his political savvy. After all, to land the second highest office in the nation six years into the political career is no small feat. And I don't know of anyone, and that includes the professional Nixon-haters (of which there are more than a few), who couldn't help but admire his comeback victory in 1968. He had pulled off the impossible, and then just as improbably, it was all thrown away.

Quite a strong argument was made charging that our system of justice was seriously compromised when Nixon and Agnew avoided having to account for their actions. In good conscience, it's hard to refute that charge. It could be argued that Nixon acted out of a misguided sense of loyalty to his subordinates, but Agnew's acceptance of money in the vice-president's office can't be seen as anything other than the criminal act that it was. As a Republican, I regret having to make such a statement;

having met Mr. Agnew a few times and admired him tremendously, I regret it even more. As vice presidents go, he was certainly no Throttlebottom. His blasts against the mobocracy of the sixties, the bias of the TV news departments, and the members of congress who had grown fainthearted because of that presence had me singing his praises. I have no doubt that had he not been hoisted on his own petard, he could easily have been elected to the presidency in 1976. In its own way, having to live with that reality every day for the rest of his life must surely be a greater punishment than anything our judicial system could have imposed on him.

My final thoughts about that sad period in our recent history are of Messrs. Woodward and Bernstein. For the tenacity of their investigative efforts and the political reforms that were ultimately the result of those efforts, I raise my hand in salute. For the depravity of their subsequent book on the private life of the Nixons and the near-fatal effect it had on Mrs. Nixon, I offer them the back of that same hand. That anyone would be sleazy enough to write such a thing and that a publishing house should want to profit by it strikes me as far more shocking than any details that might have been found within. I understand that Mr. Bernstein's former wife has published an account of their marriage. I would say no more on the matter other than I also understand that Mr. Bernstein has cried "foul" and demanded script approval of the upcoming version of it. One can only hope that if he is finding it a bit uncomfortable having his private life exposed to the world as tabloid fare, he might give some thought to those who were put in the same position by him, but without his ability to control the ensuing image.

Now in the long view of history, every political movement has taken about an equal share of ups and downs. In the aftermath of Watergate, I began to wonder if conservatism was destined to be the movement of all downs. Had one Ronald Wilson Reagan not been on the scene to rally our efforts, that cold thought might well have proven true.

I can claim a friendship with our fortieth president dating back to his first term as president of the Screen Actors Guild. There was a strong liaison between the executive boards of SAG and the MPA, and through that association, I was able to see that Ronnie's tireless efforts were, to a great extent, responsible for the Kremlinites' limited influence in that union.

Although the communism issue had us working together on a number of occasions, Ronnie and I were on opposite sides of the fence when it came to politics. By the time we met, I had lost all my enthusiasm for the New Deal that he was so fervently advocating. Nor was he alone in that pursuit. I still have a picture that I clipped from a newspaper showing Helen Gahagan Douglas flanked on a speaker's platform by Ronnie and Roy Brewer. I'm not sure which picture gives me the bigger chuckle today—that one, or one of me campaigning for Norman Thomas.

By the time the Kennedy/Nixon election rolled around, both Roy and Ronnie had become permanently disenchanted with the illusory panaceas of liberalism. Ronnie became very active in some local Republican causes which often resulted in our working together again. But it was the '64 presidential campaign that was to give us our closest association.

On the night that Barry Goldwater accepted the GOP nomination at the Cow Palace, Ronnie and I took the train from San Francisco back to Los Angeles. Jostling our way through the crowded terminal in San Francisco that night had all the appeal and much of the danger of looking for a contact lens on the floor of Macy's bargain basement the day after Christmas. Our reward for actually making it on the train was a seven hour trip, but neither of us was complaining. If anything, his dislike of flying is even more pronounced than my own. How he's managed to conquer it to meet the constant demands of his office, I couldn't say, but he certainly had a stouter heart than mine.

With "Extremism in the defense of liberty . . ." ringing in our ears throughout that long train trip, both of us were too charged up to sleep. Ronnie said that he wanted to get involved in the campaign, but he was worried that some rather strong anti-Goldwater statements that he had made several years earlier while he was still a Democrat might be an embarrassment to Barry. I was quick to assure him that I didn't feel that this would be the case, and a call to Barry the next day corroborated that Mr. Reagan's involvement in the campaign would be most welcome.

Starting after Labor Day, Ronnie and I appeared at a number of Goldwater rallies. I would introduce him, and he would deliver the sort of socko speech that he does so well. I have read several accounts that had me as the author of that famous speech that he delivered on television. That was undoubtedly the greatest speech that I have ever heard—and that's taking an awful lot of years into consideration. I would give almost anything if I could claim to be the author, but the honor is not mine.

Shortly after the election, about one hundred of us who had worked for Barry met at a local hotel to lick our wounds and do some grousing—and there was much to grouse about. There was the sabotage by the establishment; the phony story the media ran about the interview in which Barry was alleged to have said he would use nuclear weapons to end the Vietnam war; and finally the democratic charge that the GOP nominees were bigots who looked down on all except WASPs. That was incredible nonsense, of course, with Barry of Jewish ancestry and his running mate, Miller, a Catholic. But it proved the value of the Big Lie if repeated often enough.

That was our mood until Ronnie got up to speak. He said, "We've lost a battle, not a war. What this campaign was all about was a fight against Big Government, and we've made a start. We lost, but we're on our way, and if we stick together, it won't be long before we can show victory." That sounds like a cliche, I know, but when Mr. R. had finished we were all on our feet cheering.

Transferring my exultation to the typewriter, I wrote a column about "The Speech," and more importantly, about the man who gave it. Several people who were later to form the "kitchen cabinet" have told me that the column went a long way in helping to convince Ronnie that he should seek office. It's conceivable that my column might someday be awarded a higher honor than that, but at the moment, I can't see how.

If Ronald Reagan had done nothing else in his political career, the defeat that he handed our governor (1958-1966), Edmund G. (Pat) Brown, would still earn him admission into the conservative Valhalla. As with all true liberals, Pat operated under the assumption that the Ten Commandments were fine as far as they went, but a Thousand Commandments would be one hundred times better. (The Lord meant well, it seems, but he didn't have the good offices of the ADA to guide him.)

Of Ronnie's campaign for governor—where he defeated Pat Brown by over a million votes—one incident stands out. Reagan was invited by a group of GOP incumbents to address them at the Angeleno country club. He came, they saw, and he conquered. Though they were all from other states, they realized they had a good man, and Ronnie was praised lavishly.

Then a brouhaha erupted. One Demo spokesman said the club had no Jews in its membership, and that, to some, made Reagan a bigot. I'll never forget Nancy Reagan, then unused to political skullduggery, weeping at the charge. I did my best to comfort her and said, "Look, Nancy, nobody who knows Ronnie will put any credence in that."

A few days later it developed that Ronnie was not a member of the club—golf is not his cup of tea—but that Pat Brown played there regularly. Pat became a laughingstock with the boomerang. He wouldn't have won anyhow, but that sneaky punch cost him thousands of votes.

In the interregnum between the election and Reagan's installation as governor, lame duck Pat Brown proved himself anything but a gracious loser. There were, as usual when the guards are to be changed, some one hundred important posts to be filled, mainly among the judiciary. Traditionally, the outgoing executive took advantage of his final days by appointing about half, thus paying off some political debts to old cronies, and leaving the rest for the incoming administration.

But a spiteful Pat went the whole hog so that, when Reagan went to the cupboard, it was barer than Old Mother Hubbard's. Indeed, Pat even appointed to the bench two ultra-liberals his own advisors had cautioned him against: the popular saying about them was that they weren't card-carrying Communists, they were cheating the party out of dues. At any rate, they appeared regularly at C.P. fund-raising galas and were lavishly praised by the Red press, which, especially since Reagan's testimony before the HUAC, always referred to him as a "Fascist."

I joshed Reagan about the Brown appointments, and he grinned wryly and said, "I've always been a careful driver, but now I'm watching even more. Pat's arranged it so I doubt I can even fix a parking ticket."

When Ronnie took over in Sacramento, his obligations there, and his activities thereafter, were to keep him a very busy man. We corresponded and spoke on the telephone occasionally, but the reunions that we were planning always ended up being canceled for one reason or another. Because of our conflicting schedules, there was an interval of about ten years when I didn't see him. When we did meet again, it happened entirely by chance at Drucker's Barber Shop in Beverly Hills. We both have been the regular customers there for over forty years, but the only time it has ever worked out since his first election that we were there together happened a few days before Ronnie defeated the young Lochinvar from Georgia. Ronnie was just leaving as I was entering, which only gave us a moment to exchange surprised greetings before the Secret Service whisked him away.

It was quite a kick to see him again, and naturally I wished that we could have some time together, but when the responsibilities of a national campaign were considered, I was happy to have been able to see him at all. A few days after the election—when my feet were just beginning to return to the floor—Ronnie's secretary called with word that her boss would like to drop in if it would be all right. Summoning up the bogus airs of one who receives heads of state on a regular basis, I assured her that I could work it into my schedule. This precipitated the arrival of a platoon of Secret Service agents and very shortly afterward, the president-elect of the United States of America himself.

We had a long and wonderful talk that afternoon. I was thrilled for Ronnie and nearly beside myself at having the good fortune to momentarily bask in his honor. More than anything else, though, I was happy for the vindication of all the conservatives who had struggled for so long and against such incredible odds to bring about the opportunity for a turnaround that the Reagan victory signalled for America.

A few weeks later, from the comfort of my easy chair, I lifted a glass of champagne to the inaugural proceedings on the television.

Sometimes, dreams do come true.

CHAPTER TEN

Both boy and man, I have always believed in saving the best for last. When I pick up a newspaper, the first thing I do is put the sports section aside in hopes that it will assuage the distress that usually comes from reading the editorials. Place a bowl of fruit cocktail in front of me and I'll reflexively push the cherries together to save that last extra-sweet spoonful, a reward within a reward if you will.

There has been a professional application to this practice of self-parsed rewards as well, and I'm indebted to Frank Adams, Herbert Bayard Swope, and George Kaufman for teaching me one of the most important rules of writing—the Big Finish. I'm also indebted, in turn, to each of those gentlemen for teaching me the importance of not running long, and since I'm beginning to feel the celestial presence of my distinguished mentors looking over my shoulder, I'd like to wrap up this remembrance with the biggest finish that I could offer: my family.

In the early years of television, there was a popular New York-based detective melodrama that began its weekly episodes with an announcer's somber intonation: "There are eight million stories in the naked city, and this is one of them." Had the producers of that series wanted to present the most far-fetched, improbable story in the entire history of New York, it would undoubtedly be the one in which a beautiful long-stemmed Nebraska cornflower named Mary House came to Manhattan and married a short, balding, myopic comedy writer from Washington Heights named Morrie Ryskind. Having spent most of my adulthood pondering that incredible stroke of good fortune, I still don't pretend to understand it any more than I do the financial theories of John Kenneth Galbraith, but there it is, it actually did happen, and as of this writing, Mary and I have been married for fifty-five years.

The success of our half-century-plus marriage must be attributed entirely to Mary. Let's face it, this business of holy matrimony is a dicey enterprise even under the best of conditions, which automatically rules out living with a writer. Factor my foibles, allergies, aversions, and mechanical ineptitude into the equation, and I think you'll agree that Mary's forbearance makes even Caesar's wife look like a harlot.

For openers the Fates decided to celebrate my marriage proposal by sending the stock market into its storied crash. After that, the frequent theatrical outings and expensive dinners that had been the mainstay of our yearlong courtship gave away to evenings at the movies— on the infrequent occasions when I could come up with the necessary 50 cents. I was working on the script of *Strike Up the Band* at the same time, but the outcome of the project carried a great deal of uncertainty (and no advances) with it. Even if the financing, which had become very doubtful with the crash, could be finalized, there was no guarantee that audiences would like it any better in its second outing than they had in the original production. Under those conditions, I wouldn't have been surprised if Mary had called off the engagement or at least postponed the wedding, but this wondrous beauty who was turning more heads by walking into a party or down a theater aisle than any other woman in New York wouldn't hear of it. We were married in December as planned, and as Mary had predicted, *Strike Up the Band* was a hit when it opened a few weeks later. (With that kind of confidence backing me, how could it not have been?)

I was equally grateful to Mary for making the move from New York to California when my hayfever threatened to do me in altogether. By then, Mary had come to love New York with a passion that exceeded my own, and while the idea of moving to Beverly Hills might not seem like much of a sacrifice, I pray you not to confuse the city of today with the town we rolled into in 1935. Actually, village would be the more appropriate word, because it certainly did have a country crossroads atmosphere about it. It was small, all of the merchants would greet you on a first-name basis, and leaving it in any direction meant passing through dusty potato fields. It was a good life to be sure, but its isolation also made it a lonely place for the wives of newcomers without an established circle of friends.

Getting from one place to another in Los Angeles was another problem that ultimately fell on Mary. Unlike the grid layout of New York's streets, which can be negotiated so easily in a taxi (except when it rains), Los Angeles' far-flung distances (often referred to as galactic) mandate the use of a private automobile. My solution was to purchase one and hire a man to pilot us around the sun-drenched thoroughfares. Having a car and driver at my beck and call made me feel very much the pseudo-patrician, but with my mechanical dexterity being negligible if not altogether nonexistent, I would never had jeopardized the public's safety (especially in those pre-automatic transmission days) by attempting to maneuver anything as potentially dangerous as an automobile.

When we were forced to cut back on our expenses after I was shanghaied from the Good Ship Lollipop in 1947, the Cadillacs gave way to a succession of Studebakers and Chevys, and the driver was replaced by Mary, and later by the kids, with yours truly riding in the passenger seat like a cub scout being driven to his pack meeting.

On the happy subject of my children, I'd like to correct a recent *Who's Who* which had me listed as the father of three. Unless Mary had one that she has kept secret from me all these years, our omnibus stands at two, our daughter, Ruth, and our son, Allan.

If I have learned nothing else in this lifetime, I have come to know that success in life is measured not by career achievements, but by the well-being of one's children. In that respect, I consider myself to be a very successful man. Both Ruth and Allan have done very well for themselves, and have done so (a little extra frosting on the cake here) as writers. Ruth, who managed to attain one of the goals that alluded me, a degree from Columbia, lives in New York, where she is the executive editor of the *Journal of American Cardiologists*. Allan, who pulled a hitch in the army before attending college and graduate school, lives in Washington, DC, where he is the co-owner and editor of *Human Events*—which has been my sounding board for the last few years.

That our kids turned out so well is, of course, another miracle which can only be chalked up to Mary. I did my best, which will, I trust, stop any sort of "Morrie Dearest" revenge, but the bulk of the upbringing was supervised by Mary. And I warrant you, it is no easy task to impart normal standards and values in a community like Beverly Hills where it was not unusual for their playmates' birthday parties to cost $15,000 (and this was in the forties!).

Despite Mary's best intentions to the contrary, Allan came to be inexorably linked to the opulent folklore of Beverly Hills. What made this such a hoot is that it came through his membership, of all things, in Cub Scout Pack 77, of which, incidentally, Mary was the den mother. The Scouts fielded an excellent Little League team with Allan as catcher, Joe Blatchford as pitcher, and Bill Warren covering second base. The trio were as inseparable as Athos, Parthos, and Aramis, both on and off the field, and even today, despite widely divergent political leanings, they remain as close as brothers. (Joe grew up to become director of the Peace Corps under Richard Nixon, and Bill—we're still not certain how this happened—became active in liberal Democratic circles and served as campaign manager to Eugene McCarthy and Gore Vidal.)

However, one Saturday afternoon when baseball occupied the most important place in their lives, Allan sprained his ankle sliding into home plate. In spite of his injury, he insisted on making the rounds of his Sunday morning paper route. I had tried to talk him out of taking the job in the first place, but he was determined to show me that he could make his own pocket money the way I had when I used to get up and work twelve hours in the steel mill, chop a cord of wood, and milk twenty cows before walking barefoot through the snow those thirty miles to school. (Well, what father hasn't exaggerated about his youthful hardships?)

Allan could barely walk on the morning after his injury, let alone ride his bicycle, so I had our driver get up early and take him around his route. Not exactly Horatio Alger in the classic sense of the legend, but I certainly admired his spunk. Our car (this was in our milk and honey days) was a limousine, and that's how Beverly Hills—and what a kick Fred Allen got out of this—came to have a chauffeur-driven paper boy.

Mary's high standards of child rearing were instilled in her by her father, Dr. Julius House, a remarkable man, and truly one of the last of the American pioneers. Dr. House dedicated his life to education, and among the many accomplishments of his long career was the founding of Kingfisher University in Oklahoma when it was still the Indian Territory. To enroll his students, he would drive through the farmlands in his horse-and-buggy asking whether anyone had a youngster who wanted to go to college. And for those not yet ready for the advanced curriculum, he ran a preparatory academy—roughly the equivalent of the last two years of high school.

In addition to running the schools, Dr. House also taught Greek, Latin, and English—and apparently well, as two of his students won Rhodes Scholarships. A while back, I met one of his distinguished charges who had gone on to become a full professor at the University of Maryland. It was with a great deal of fondness that she recalled her mentor and the days under his stern tutelage at Kingfisher. Had the university not been founded, the harsh circumstances and isolation of her prairie life (before attending Kingfisher, she had never used any comb other than the ones her father had fashioned from the horns of his cattle) would never have allowed her the opportunity to continue her education beyond the local one-room schoolhouse.

Being a man of the West, Dr. House had little regard for New York and the accelerated pace of metropolitan life. He surprised us, though, during one of his rare visits to the city by asking to see a speakeasy. You have to understand that this was a man who had taken one drink in his entire life. The drink was a glass of sherry. He rather liked it, and for that reason immediately swore off the stuff for good. Stern folks out there on the plains.

It happened that *Of Thee I Sing*—the reason for Dr. House's visit—had pulled Mary and me out of debt, and we decided to celebrate by throwing a "solvency" party at "21," which also took care of Dr. House's speakeasy request. We invited all of our friends, which turned out to be a big mistake as it put Dr. House in the same room with Groucho—sort of Mr. Chips meets Captain Spaulding. Early in the evening, Dr. House was speaking with Morrie Ernst about a case that had recently been decided by the Supreme Court. When the phrase "abortion of justice" fell on Groucho sitting at the next table, it naturally couldn't pass without a comment. "Say," said Groucho, face aglow, "speaking of abortions, I'm looking for someone to perform my next one."

This brought a slight gasp from Morrie and a cold stare from Dr. House that sent Groucho—momentarily—back to his table. When "abortion of justice" was again mentioned, Groucho came back with "And if you know one that gives you group rates, I've got a couple of brothers that will keep him in business the rest of his life."

Party or not, that sort of effrontery was not to be tolerated by the Nebraska academician. Drawing up a look of intimidation honed to the paralyzing perfection on thousands of pupils, he turned to Groucho and snapped, "Young man, you will sit there, and you will be quiet for the rest of the evening."

The party came to a complete stop at that point as all eyes turned to Groucho, who slumped in his chair absolutely speechless. It was the first and last time that I witnessed the phenomenon.

Dr. House's principal opinion about politics was that it should be a very private matter. All in all, that's probably a very sensible opinion, but it was one that Mary didn't share with her father. I was thought to be the corrupting influence on her, but the truth of the matter is that it was Mary who often pulled me into an active participation with the body politic.

The first of our joint political ventures was on behalf of Fiorello LaGuardia's 1933 mayoral campaign in New York. LaGuardia was really bucking the odds by taking on Tammany Hall with his fusion ticket, but after Jimmy Walker's mayoralty went down in ashes the previous year, the public was ready for a change, and the "Little Flower" pulled off the impossible.

Mary worked tirelessly at the LaGuardia headquarters as a volunteer, and she too pulled off a seemingly impossible feat by getting George Kaufman involved in the campaign. Although George had little regard for politics other than as a juicy target for satire, he always had a high regard for Mary's opinion. Indeed, it was on Mary's recommendation that Bill Gaxton had the sort of sex appeal that would lure women to *Of Thee I Sing* that George cast him as Wintergreen.

LaGuardia was such a warm and effusive person that even his opponents were charmed by him. George and I fell under his spell as soon as we were introduced, and in hopes of making some sort of contribution to his election, we wrote and performed some mock debates on the radio. Whether they swayed any votes, I rather doubt, but it was great fun. When we wrote *A Night at the Opera*, we named Chico's character Fiorello. A dubious honor, I must say, but Hizzoner was pretty tickled by it, and every time he visited California he would stop at the house to say hello.

After we moved to California, the responsibilities of raising two children forced Mary to channel all of her time and energy into domestic concerns. But even here, one of her tangential involvements was to have political ramifications of a serious nature.

Heeding the example of her father, Mary—who received her B.A. from the University of Chicago when she was eighteen—had long been involved in education. During the course of one of her terms as president of the Beverly Hills PTA, Mary hosted an afternoon envelope-stuffing session of school curricula here at the house. One of the ladies assisting her that day was the wife of a well-known writer who would later play a significant role in the controversy that nearly tore Hollywood apart. At one point the lady turned to Mary and casually asked, "How old are you?" Now it has been my observation that revealing one's age is not a particularly favorite pastime in feminine circles, but after a reflexive gasp or two, Mary fessed up. This brought a round of chuckles from the ladies. "No, no, dear," said the lady who had so brazenly asked the question, "I don't mean your actual age. How old are you in the (Communist) party? I'm three-years-old myself." This was the first indication that we had of the CP existence in Hollywood; regretfully, it wasn't our last.

When World War II broke out, the Ryskinds proudly did their part. I stayed out of everybody's way, and Mary joined the Interception Command. This was the civilian branch of the Army Air Corps that identified and tracked the movements of all aircraft flying in southern California, one of the most vital and vulnerable areas of the country during the war.

Mary joined up right after Pearl Harbor, when the threat of an invasion on the West Coast was a very real possibility. "Loose lips sink ships" was the prevailing spirit then, and no one honored the vow of secrecy more scrupulously than Mary. For a year-and-a-half, I had no idea where she went or what she did every time she donned her uniform and reported for duty. On the day that I confronted her with details of where her operation was and what went on there, her face flushed with alarm. Before she began conjuring up images of a blindfold and last cigarette for inadvertently revealing top-secret information, I eased her out of her worries by showing her the photo layout of the Interceptor Command's camouflaged headquarters in that week's edition of *Life Magazine*.

The war against the Axis powers ended at the time our children were beginning their wars with adolescence. I'm not sure which was the harder on Mary, but it's nice to report that she again came through victorious. When she finally had some free time to herself I expected her to devote it to leisurely activities, but as soon as Ruth and Allan flew the nest, politics once more took over Mary's life. In '62 she was a precinct worker for Richard Nixon, in '64 she ran George Murphy's Beverly Hills precinct office, and in '66 she really outdid herself.

That was the year—from mid-August onward—when I suddenly found I was married to a career woman whose one purpose in life was supervising some one hundred local precincts on behalf of the candidacy of a certain movie actor. She would leave early and come home late, and I caught only occasional glimpses of her.

It was, I hoped, just a passing infatuation, and I decided to treat it as a man of the world. I uttered no reproaches but threw myself into my own work. That is, I endeavored to—but the phone rang incessantly with strange men demanding Mary's whereabouts. Luckily, she had left two phone numbers at which she could be reached. Many's the night, you must realize, when I wept myself to sleep wondering about meetings to which I was never invited.

The worst thing about the situation was that it turned me, willy-nilly, into a sort of housekeeper, a job for which I was inadequately prepared. If a light went out, I had no idea where the extra bulbs were kept, so that gradually the house was plunged into almost total darkness, and I could work at my typewriter only by a candlelight.

There was the time a pipe burst, and I tried to clean up the mess as best I could and left a note for Mary asking her what to do about it. Her memo—slipped under my door—was terse: "Wait till after the election."

Then came the rains and the roof began to leak. I spread paper all over the floors and left another pleading note. The answer was sharp this time: "If I've told you once I've told you a hundred times not to bother me till after the election."

I had visions of the house drifting away, and I prayed that it would float past Reagan's headquarters so I could wave a last goodbye at her, even if she only called back, "Wait till after the election."

Naturally she could do no shopping during this period, and I got my meals by a systematic attack on the pantry and refrigerator—both well stocked. But in the long siege, I ate my way through all the mint jelly, chutney, canned soups, tuna, dietetic ice cream, and fig newtons. Toward the end I began to budget myself on a few raw onions, the last of the sardines, and a dill pickle.

On the very last day of my ordeal I could find nothing—absolutely nothing—but ice cubes in the refrigerator. Ingenuity is the mother of invention, so I defrosted the ice cubes, heated them, and then went to the lemon tree in our back yard, pulled off the one remaining lemon and squeezed the juice into the ice cubes. It would have been better with sugar, but that had long vanished. Luckily, this happened to be the day that Ronald Reagan retired Pat Brown. The next day, Mary was home to restore the larder and cook me a fine spanking breakfast, which was most welcome, although the results of the preceding day had left me in such a euphoric state that I might easily have been able to continue existing solely on atmosphere.

Now, as I've stated earlier, I'm still pondering why this intelligent, accomplished, highly respected woman has blessed me with so many years of unflagging support, especially in light of the succession of faux pas that I have notched up over the years. (And, oh, how my *pas* have *fauxed*!)

Let's begin with my gambling. I have long since ceased to follow the sport of kings, but when I was a regular out at Hollywood Park, it was not unusual for total strangers to come up and politely ask me to mark my choices for them—which they would thereupon avoid like the plague. It seems that on that unforgettable day when Willie Shoemaker established a track record by riding eight mounts and bringing six of them into the winner's circle, I created something of a record myself. The only times I bet on Wee Willie that day was when he rode his two losers, which made me the only person at the track who didn't get to the payoff window. These stories have a way of getting around, and I have had horse owners plead tearfully with me not to bet on their entries.

While my Runyonesque notoriety in local horse-racing circles was considerable, my reputation as a card player was even worse—worse beyond my wildest dreams. In fact, I can truthfully state that my exploits at poker were known worldwide.

You see, for years I was a member of the Hoyle Club. This was a friendly get-together organized by that celebrated actor and ardent advocate of the Sixteenth Amendment's repeal, Charles Coburn. Charlie had two great passions in his life, Shakespeare and poker, and could come up with an appropriate quotation from the Bard whether he won or lost a pot.

Although the Hoyle Club was organized by an actor, our membership was mostly comprised of writers. George Kaufman, Moss Hart, Marc Connelly, Howard Lindsay, and Russel Crouse always joined us when they were in town, and with such a distinguished group of authors seated at one table, it was inevitable that I would be dubbed the "Pulitzer Prize Loser."

Especially memorable in this vein was that round when six hands were dealt, but after a dozen or so raises before the draw, only Crouse, Coburn, and myself remained. Crouse stood pat while Coburn and I each drew two. Crouse bet out; I found that I had drawn the fourth eight, which brought anticipatory spasms of breaking even for the first time in years, so I raised. Coburn reraised. After about the tenth raise, Crouse dropped his straight and some fine old Anglo-Saxon invectives, leaving me alone to face the monocled libertarian. Charles and I went at it, and after another hot session of raises I not only felt sorry for my old friend, but I realized that he might have four nines, so I called. Coburn stayed on the king, jack, and ten of hearts, and had drawn the ace and queen of that suit for a royal straight flush. It could only happen once in a million times, and then, only to me.

To prevent the asphyxiation of our families from all the tobacco smoke that was generated at our sessions, we held our games at the Players Club. To anyone familiar with Hollywood folklore, that name will be remembered as the millstone that ruined Preston Sturges—certainly one of the greatest comedy filmmakers in the history of motion pictures (one of his classics being *The Lady Eve* in which Charlie Coburn gave such a grand performance as an aging card shark).

Preston made a fortune as a writer-director (At one point he was the third-highest salaried man in America.), all of which was lost to the bad management and sticky fingers of his staff at the Players. Later he was to be at odds with the studio bosses who refused to grant him the complete artistic control of his films that he so fully deserved. With no prospects for future work in Hollywood, and without any sort of financial cushion thanks to the Players, he was forced to look for work in Europe where the pickings were equally lean. The Players, by the way, is still up there on the Sunset Strip. It's a Japanese restaurant now, and although it's silly to hold a grudge against a building, I still can't go past it without recalling the brilliant career that was lost because of it.

Nor can I pass the place without recalling the blaze of publicity that surrounded our last game there. It all started out innocently enough when we met for our monthly get-together. I'd like to reiterate that ours was a friendly quarter-ante game with a dollar limit on the bets. The record for a one-night loss was $50, and guess who the distinction belonged to? But there were a number of speakeasy-type gambling clubs operating around the Strip then, where $50 was the ante and losses of $50,000 were the norm.

One night—and how could it not have been the night of our monthly game—two plainclothes deputies were sent out to investigate one of those high-roller games operating near the Players Club. Finding the premises dark, they acted on a tip, and a few minutes later they were standing over our table.

Charles Coburn looked up when the lawmen walked into the room, and with his customary tactfulness asked, "What the hell is this?" Stamped apparently from the Jack Webb mould, the ranking detective said nothing as he laid his badge on the table. "So what?" said Charles as he laid his honorary badge on the table beside it. "I often play cards with the sheriff." At that point the lawmen got very red-faced and apologetic as they recognized Charles. Unfortunately, having earlier peeked into the upstairs room where we played and seen the game in progress, they had already phoned in for backup, which arrived momentarily in a crescendo of wailing sirens. There was nothing they could do to undo the process at that point, so the $17 worth of chips in the pot (a figure indelibly etched in my memory) was confiscated as evidence and we were ordered to appear at a judge's office the next afternoon.

The next morning, as Mary and I were having a big laugh over the whole thing, Charles called to say that we needn't bother reporting to the judge's chamber. His attorney would appear for us, pay the fine in camera, and there would be no publicity about the matter. The judge, it seems, was also a poker player.

When Mary and Ruth returned from doing some shopping that afternoon, they brought back a late edition of the *Herald* for me. Apparently, it had been a slow news day, because under the blaring front page headline: "Coburn, Ryskind Arrested In Gambling Raid," were pictures of Charles and yours truly. And this was only a prelude to the wire services picking it up and putting it out over the whole country—with the details becoming more exaggerated with each retelling. By the time *Newsweek* ran it, the $17 in chips had grown to $25,000 in cash, which was fitting, I suppose, as their cover story was on inflation; and by the time the story ran in England and Europe it had grown to $50,000 in cash.

For a while, it seemed that we would never be able to shed our "Public Enemy Number One" status, nor did Charles, who absolutely reveled in our notoriety, want to. By the time the whole thing did blow over, he had two scrapbooks filled with front-page articles of our escapade, and that Christmas he sent out greeting cards with a picture of him dressed in a striped convict's uniform.

What I regretted most about the incident was losing the Hoyle Club. Because of all the publicity, Preston Sturges received a sanction against any further gambling taking place at the Players. The last thing that any of us wanted to do was add to his burden, so a succession of new meeting places were tried. For various reasons, we were never able to find a spot that served our purpose, and soon after, the Hoyle Club was disbanded.

Thereafter my gambling impulses were limited to occasional trips to Las Vegas, where my luck held unswervingly to form. On my last visit there I watched a roulette wheel for an hour and noted that the number nine hadn't shown up. Being a keen student of the law of probabilities, I invested a silver dollar on that number, and again, it failed to appear. I was not discouraged; 399 more times I put a silver dollar on nine, skipping dinner in the process, and it still hadn't come in. By that time, I couldn't afford dinner, nor could I any longer afford not to acknowledge that I wasn't destined to be the new

Nicky Arnstein, and so ended my career as a man of chance.

Embarrassing though they were, I'm afraid that my ill-fated gambling exploits were only a small part of the reason that the good ladies of Beverly Hills were constantly shaking their heads in sadness and tsk-tsking, "Poor Mary." You see, socially I was even more left-footed.

Illustrative of why those good B.H. ladies were also wont to repeat things such as "She just can't take him anywhere," would be our standing with—let's call them the Blanks out of respect for the living. The Blanks live right around the corner and are old and dear friends of ours—except during election campaigns. They voted for Roosevelt the four times his name appeared on the ballot, and the next couple of times after that they wrote it in out of habit. But, as long as you don't discuss religion or politics and just stick to bridge, they are as nice a couple as you would care to meet. I happen to love bridge, and I never discuss religion. Politics, well that's a different matter.

Take for instance our initial meeting on that Sunday afternoon all those years ago, when they threw a party in their garden to welcome us to the community. It was a beautiful February day with clear skies and balmy breezes, and it was a beautiful garden with fragrant flowers and topiary statuettes. In fact, everything was beautiful, including my disposition, which would have remained so had it not been for that serpent. Must they (and alas! they must) be forever spoiling gardens?

This one came in the guise of a $3,000 a week writer who was later to figure prominently in the communism brouhaha. Ensconced on a chaise lounge with his drink often refreshed from a waiter's tray, he waxed euphoric all through the afternoon about the glories of Stalin's collectivization program. For Mary's sake, I held my tongue through the first hour of it and most of the second one too. But we all have our breaking point, and with the third hour of his harangue approaching, I couldn't resist observing that my distinguished colleague did indeed

seem to be dedicated to the world's struggle, and I was
sure that in his heart of hearts he would rather be standing united with all those happy Marxists in a sub-zero
Moscow breadline instead of lolling around in the California sunshine, but then "perhaps they also serve who sit
and are waited upon."

The party took quite a different turn after that, and
after that it was a good dozen years before the Blanks
invited us back for anything but bridge. A great deal can
happen in twelve years, a great deal of which being the
sort of things that aren't discussed at bridge. So how was
I to know that they had just come into some money and
gone in for some trendy sort of analysis—a subject which
can set me off faster than politics?

True, I did have some apprehensions as we entered,
but that was only because I didn't recognize any of the
other guests, and I am shy about strangers. Not sensitive,
just shy. But the Blanks greeted us effusively, the butler
they had hired for the occasion pressed a martini on us,
and everything seemed hunky-dory.

I was on my third martini before I realized that the
other guests were six assorted psychiatrists and analysts—
I know there's a technical difference, but don't ask me
what—and their wives. What tipped me off was the conversation, which finally got around, as it inevitably does,
to the movies. One of the psychiatrists was holding forth
on the psychoanalytical aspects of Olivier's *Hamlet*, and I
gathered that he approved enthusiastically. I also gathered, although he didn't actually come out and say so,
that he wasn't taken in by any of the idiotic notions that
any of those various claimants had written the plays attributed to Shakespeare. He knew who had written them:
Sigmund Freud.

Now as a good Shakespearean, I hold that Shakespeare
wrote Shakespeare, and I am normally prepared to give
battle for my theory. But to allay, once and for all, Mrs.
Blank's strange delusion that I don't know how to behave
at parties, I said nothing and accepted another martini

from the butler, a stout fellow who believed in giving an honest day's work for an honest day's pay. This time I took an olive instead of an onion. They were mighty good olives too—our own California brand—which led me to have two or three more, which in turn reinforced another theory of mine that only people with inferiority complexes have to talk to prove they're important. At the moment, the only thing I was suffering from was an exquisite sense of euphoria. In my generous mood, I was even willing to listen to a theory that Rocky Graziano had written the odes of Q. H. Flaccus. One more olive, indeed, and I would have promulgated the theory myself.

Things went along swimmingly for about an hour. What pulled me under was that psychoanalyst's wife who turned to me during a lull and asked whether I had seen the Olivier *Hamlet*. Mary was watching me intently, so all I said was "Yes." Mary beamed. Ah, if that had been the end of it.

But Freudians, apparently, are like sharks, in that they must be forever moving or die. "And how did you like it?" continued the lady man-eater.

"Very much," I said, "though I didn't think it was as good as his *Henry V*. That, I thought, was brilliant."

There was blood in the water now. "You mean to say," she said with a sneer that revealed several rows of razor-sharp teeth, "you actually preferred his *Henry* to his *Hamlet*?" She stopped, but I had the eerie feeling that my peril was only beginning. Looking around, I saw why: other sharks, the antennae of their ilk on red alert, began to circle.

I don't want to overdramatize, but it was a tense moment: a dozen psychoanalysts, fins and jaws poised, against one man armed only with a clear conscience and a half-a-dozen martinis. This, definitely, was it. I've always wondered how I would act at the Final Curtain—pleading and snivelling like a coward, or smiling and defiant in the tradition of Nathan Hale and Alan Ladd. Let it be recorded that my boots stayed on. I said "Yes."

"Hmph," snorted the psychocuda on my left, "that's revealing."

"Very revealing," the others chorused and exchanged knowing looks.

For the first time that evening I was disconcerted. I didn't know what I had revealed, but from the way they were smiling at each other, I knew it was something dirty that had come up from my subconscious. But what? A misplaced libido? A floating id? My whole life passed before me in the twinkling of an eye, and there were some things I didn't want anybody to know.

My concern must have shown itself, for a great white in the corner rose from his chair, and kept rising to his full height (big enough to scare even Hemingway, was my hasty calculation), and pressed his advantage. "And just what didn't you like about it?"

"I didn't say I didn't like it," I replied, "I merely said I thought *Henry V* was better."

There were hoots of "emotional grandeur," and "anti-social tendencies." A lady mako whipped out her note-book and climbed on the lap of the great white, who immediately began dictating his clinical observation to her.

They were circling for the kill, but I stood my ground. "I didn't say I didn't like it," I repeated, "but since you ask me, I was puzzled by the kiss Hamlet gave Gertrude. It wasn't a filial kiss—it was definitely sexual."

The other hushed, but the tall one continued. "And what's puzzling about that?"

"Well," I said, "you don't kiss your mother like that, do you? Now if it had been Ophelia, I'd understand. But your own mother?"

"Now that," said the psychocuda who had started the whole thing, "is even more revealing. In fact, outside of Krafft-Ebing, a couple of cases recorded in the *Journal of Abnormal Psychology*, and the last issue of *Confidential*, that's about the most revealing thing I've ever heard."

There, I'd done it again; I had revealed myself. And then the questions flew at me from all sides: "Didn't you ever read *Hamlet*?" "Don't you know he hated his uncle because he loved Gertrude himself?" "What do you think Shakespeare meant by the play anyhow?" "How about another martini?" (The last question was from the butler, bless him, as he handed me a fresh one. This one had both an olive and an onion, and is known as a double martini.)

"Just a second," I said, as I took a sip. Refreshed, I returned to combat. "Now, then, let's get this right. Yes, I've read *Hamlet*! And seen it, too—from Walter Hampden on the stage to Olivier in the films. As a matter of fact, after I saw the picture I went home and reread it just to see how Olivier got to the notion: and I defy you to show me one word in the text to indicate Hamlet felt that way about his mother. I did more: I discussed the point with some Shakespearean actors—Charles Coburn, for one—and they were as puzzled as I was. Mr. Coburn toured for over thirty years as a Shakespearean actor, and is steeped in Shakespearean lore; he assures me Shakespeare didn't write *Hamlet* that way, and Burbage didn't play it that way."

"Burbage-Schmurbage!" snarled a hammerhead standing by the piano. "In Germany they've been playing it that way since the turn of the century already."

"If," said the great white, rolling back his eye in preparation for the final attack, "if Hamlet wasn't in love with his mother, why did he hate Claudius enough to want to kill him?"

"Look," I said, "his father comes back from the grave, says he's been bumped off by his brother, and asks his son to avenge him. Wouldn't any son . . ."

"People don't come back from the grave," he interrupted sternly, "and anybody who pretends to have gone to college should know better. That was a daydream of Hamlet's invented by him to justify his guilt feelings about his mother."

"But Shakespeare had him come back," I cried out.

"Shakespeare never went to college."

That did it. "Nuts!" I quoted a famous American general and began to scotch sharks hip and thigh. What followed is probably best not repeated here. Merely let it be said that for quite some time—the Kennedy years to be exact—bridge and not dinner once more governed our social relationship with the Blanks.

With the coming of Camelot, the Blanks were moved to be magnanimous regarding Mary's loneliness: "Well, let's give them one more try. Maybe he'll behave himself this time." The invitation was snapped up by Mary, who thereupon put me through a Pygmalion-like refresher course on Emily Post: you know, light the ladies' cigarettes for them, the salad is on the left and, above all, no political or psychoanalytical discussions. It was a rather intensive training session, if I might say so, but I came through with flying colors, and my blessed Mary, for the first time in a dozen years, was hopeful.

Mary's good cheer was displaced at the door by the look of acute distress on Mrs. Blank's face. In an effort to reassure our hostess that tonight wouldn't be a repeat of my previous performances, I immediately began demonstrating some dazzling footwork as I ran around lighting cigarettes for everybody, male and female alike. I even remembered (from having watched innumerable Ronald Colman movies) to put my glass on a coaster and not on the piano, but this display of courtliness had no effect on Mrs. Blank, who continued to fret as though she were trapped between Scylla and Charybdis.

It wasn't until I was being introduced to a late arrival—who had just arrived back in town—that I understood the apprehension of our hostess. As we were shaking hands, I suddenly realized that this was the distinguished liberal whose views I had—what shall I say—"discussed" in a recent column. And from the glint in his eyes, it was a cinch he had read my piece.

I caught the look of fear on Mary's face and hastily struck a match for his cigarette. Unfortunately, it turned out that he didn't smoke. Still, he appeared to appreciate

the gesture. I used the match to light a cigarette for the
lady across the room and stole a glance into my corner
for further instructions. My manager made that welcome
circle with her thumb and forefinger that signifies things
are going well. And from then until dinner it was a
breeze.

The dinner, I hasten to add, was superb, as usual, and
what's more, I managed to make it all the way to the main
course without slurping, spilling, or dropping a single
thing. I was rather proud of that accomplishment, as the
conversation at the table was more or less dominated by
the celebrity guest who was expounding on one of the
basic postulates of the American liberal: that the tenets of
conservatism are arrived at by men of ill will and no
compassion, whose gods are selfishness and avarice;
whereas the liberal reaches his conclusions by a combination of pure brotherly love and superior intelligence.
There have been numerous occasions when arguments a
great deal less barbed than that one have moved me to a
pronounced state of vociferous animation, but this time
(to the great relief of our hostess) I kept my tongue by
paying strict attention to the food.

It wasn't until my third helping, when the goodliberal
(that's one word, please) switched from the general to the
specific, that I began to listen. After all, he was a widely
quoted authority, with a substantial influence on the
political philosophy that had triumphed in the previous
election. He had just returned from a fact-finding mission
abroad, but his findings had only reinforced his belief in
the liberal credo: namely, that we should give everything
we have, instead of the miserly billion we have shelled
out, to help the underdeveloped areas of the world come
to full bloom. As Mr. Luce's boys used to say: no penny-
pincher he.

Normally this too would have stimulated whatever the
jigger is that, annoyed, begins shooting quantities of hy-
drochloric acid into the system and starts the stomach
eating into itself. But here again I rose, Gandhi-like, above

the fray. And although I didn't actually come out and say
so, I was in limited agreement with the esteemed guest's
assertion. India, for instance, was then demanding to
have the dosage of its annual multi-billion dollar aid pre-
scription doubled. While the figure might indeed have
seemed high, you must remember that we had sent them
Galbraith, which gave Nehru a legitimate claim to puni-
tive damages.

Dessert was being served at that point. Had I been
able to remain silent for a few more minutes, our social
banishment might well have ended. But the distinguished
guest had one last row to hoe, concerning the National
Committee for a Sane Nuclear Policy—better known as
SANE, in accordance with our custom of calling a six-
footer Shorty and a 400-pounder Tiny.

Now, I don't say that the SANE argument isn't interesting—specious maybe, but interesting. Unlike Patrick
Henry, a noted warmonger of his day, the SANE folks
know of no way of judging the future but by completely
ignoring the past. They care no hoot whether the USSR
or the U.S. is right, nor even what is right; the important
thing to them is that the two roughnecks don't disturb
the rest of the uncommitted world, including SANE, which
has no stake in the matter. If we can find some uninhab-
ited planet on which to destroy each other, why go to it,
and a plague on both your houses.

For, unlike you and me, who are just hungering to die
in a thermonuclear flash, SANE is opposed to nuclear
war and demands peace—at almost any price. It wishes
with all its (bleeding) heart that the Soviet Union weren't
so intransigent, but since that is the case, let's be realistic.
Somebody has to give up, and since the Kremlin won't,
it's up to us. What was holding up the show, according to
the eminent liberal, was the manic regressive conservatives who were psychologically unable to face a SANE
world.

The cheesecake in front of me looked tempting, but
I had had enough. I had promised that I wouldn't discuss
politics or psychoanalysis, but a combination of the two

worked on me like one of those little rubber hammers to the patella. Before I could stop myself, I had announced, "Just a minute."

It seems I took more than a minute, and that once I was into it, my rebuttal made Cicero's reference to Cataline sound like a glowing eulogy. And I must say that my broadsides were returned double over. And once he was into it, the suave and sinistral SANE exponent turned into a firebrand that made even Castro's pyrotechnics sound like the polite utterances of a well-mannered youngster born of the happy union of Louisa May Alcott and Little Lord Fauntleroy. And in the midst of it all was my gracious, my guileless, my guilty-by-association Mary, sweetly trying to avoid a one-way ticket back to Elba with "And to think, dear, that you could top such a wonderful meal with such a marvelous dessert. You must give me the recipe."

After that free-for-all (and I can't say that it came as a surprise), our twelve years banishment was doubled, bringing us up to the present time. But soon (all's well that ends well) we shall be dining at the Blanks again. While my reputation for polarizing parties hasn't changed—nor has the Blanks' dread of setting me off— what has saved us from yet another twelve years exile is the fact that Mary and I will soon be a threat to Washington, DC, parties, and a farewell/celebration (the order is probably reversed) is called for.

With the exception of a very small circle of cherished friends, and that includes the Blanks, the old gang is no longer with us. And it's gotten to the point where I'm not only hearing the chimes at midnight, but time's winged chariot as well. Mary and I have lived out here for fifty years, forty-eight of them at 605 North Hillcrest Drive. An investment in time of that proportion builds up quite an emotional reluctance about moving on, but the desire to be with our children and grandchildren unknots all ties to the past with the nimblest of ease. My biggest regret at this point is that we haven't gotten around to it much sooner.

As Mary and I embark on our new adventure, I'd like to close this remembrance with an expression of optimism for the future. This ongoing production known as America has certainly known its share of bad performances and a couple of times has nearly had to post a closing notice. But it has never, ever been because of script problems. With the bicentennial of our constitution a whisper of time away, it's pretty thrilling to contemplate that same constitution's quadrennial celebration; and the Washingtons, Jeffersons, and Lincolns not yet born who will take center stage in their turn to ensure that that day will indeed occur. Just stick to the script, boys, there will never be a better one written.

EPILOGUE

Morrie Ryskind was enjoying good health and high spirits on 21 June 1985 when he completed the six-month-long series of weekly interviews that comprise the basis of this memoir. The following week, he and Mrs. Ryskind made their eagerly-awaited move to Washington, DC. Morrie quietly passed away on 25 August 1985, while he and Mrs. Ryskind were having breakfast. He was eighty-nine-years-and-ten-months-old.

—John Roberts

The very young **Morrie Ryskind**

Morrie Ryskind—At
Home, Relaxed

Mary Ryskind

A Family Photo: Morrie Ryskind,
his wife, Mary, daughter, Ruth,
and son, Allan

Morrie Ryskind with his perpetual love—newspapers.

Morrie and Mary Ryskind with **William F. Buckley, Jr.,** at a 1965 Beverly Hills Republican Dinner.

Morrie Ryskind with **Hedda Hopper** in a skit at a 1965 Republican Dinner. **Congressman Don Jackson** and a young **William F. Buckley, Jr.,** look on.

Ernie Pyle, celebrated war correspondent, poses with **Morrie Ryskind** on the set of *Story of G.I. Joe.*

Morrie Ryskind with **Fred Allen, Rudee Vallee, Don Ameche** and others.